**MAKING
MONEY
BEING FUNNY**

MAKING MONEY BEING FUNNY

A **Game Plan** to **Financial Security** for Comics, Writers, Content Creators & Entertainers

JUDY CARTER

MAKING MONEY BEING FUNNY
A Game Plan for Financial Security for Comics, Writers, Content Creators & Entertainers

Copyright © 2026 by Judy Carter

Printed in the United States of America.

All rights reserved. No part of this publication may be reproduced, distributed, or transmitted in any form or by any means—electronic, mechanical, photocopying, recording, or otherwise—without the prior written permission of the author or publisher, except in the case of brief quotations in reviews or critical articles.

This is a work of nonfiction. While based on real experiences, some names, details, and identifying characteristics may have been changed for privacy, clarity, or comedic effect. Any resemblance to actual persons, living or dead, is coincidental.

For permissions, workshops, keynotes, digital resources, and updates on new releases, visit: JudyCarter.com

All inquiries may be directed through the website.

Carter's Comedy Cash Formula™ and *Making Money Being Funny*™ are trademarks of Judy Carter.

ISBN (Paperback): 979-8-218-93223-7

Cover Photo: Bader Howard

Cover Design: Carin Castenlnuova-Tedesco

Interior Design: Melissa Farr, Back Porch Creative, LLC

Interior Editing: SJ Hodges

Publisher: Comedy Workshops Publishing

DEDICATION

To the comedians who still dare to tell the truth—
even when it costs them gigs, friends, or safety.

In a time when democracy trembles and censorship hides behind
civility, you stand alone with a microphone as your sword.

You remind us that laughter isn't just entertainment—
it's an act of resistance.

Keep going. The mic is mightier than the mob.

Table of Contents

👥 = Accountability Buddy Exercise　　🖳 = AI Prompt Exercise

Endorsements from the Pros xiii

Preface 1
    Which Comedy Crisis Is Yours? 1
    What If Your Passions Paid? 3

Introduction: Broke Ain't A Joke **5**
    Why Are Headlining Comics Sleeping in Their Cars? 5
    You Deserve Better (and It's Possible) 6

CHAPTER 1: Monetize Your Funny—Create Like an Artist, ... **9**
Hustle Like a CEO
    The Reality Check 9
    From Open Mics to Direct Deposits 9
    Shift Your Mindset: From Gigging Comic to 10
    Comedy Entrepreneur
    The Kevin Hart Playbook: From Gig Worker to Mogul 11

CHAPTER 2: Why the Hell Should You Listen to Me? **13**
    If I Can Make Money Being Funny, Trust Me— 13
    You Can Too
    Why I'm Telling You This Story 14
    How I Became a 10-Year-Old Mogul 15
    From Birthday Parties to Big-Girl Branding 16

CHAPTER 3: Find Your Comedy "Why" **19**
    When Comedy Wasn't a Career—It Was Survival 19
    Exercise #1: Discover Your "Why" (Hint: Fame Isn't One) 🖳 . . . 20
    Exercise #2: From Dream to Game Plan— 22
    Create Your Comedy Career Vision 🖳
    Exercise #3: Turn Your "Why" and "Vision" into Motivation 🖳 . . 25

CHAPTER 4: The Game Plan 27
   How to Use This Book 27
   Exercise #4: Find Your Accountability Buddy— 29
   The Cure for Procrastination 👥
   Exercise #5: Seal the Deal—Your Commitment to 30
   Comedy (and Yourself 👥)

CHAPTER 5: Carter's Comedy Cash Formula™ 31
   The Math Behind the Laughs—and Why It Pays to Know It 31

CHAPTER 6: Go Niche Yourself 35
   The Math Behind the Laughs—And Why It Pays toKnow It 35
   The Big Lie: Fame = Fortune 36
   The Real Goal: Become a Niche Sensation 37
   What Is and Isn't a Niche? 39

CHAPTER 7: Comic Undercover: Going Deep to Find Your Niche . 41
   The Comic FBI File—Your Funny Background Investigation . . . 41
   Exercise #6: Find Your Money-Making Niche 🔬 44

ELEMENT #1: Your Niche 65

CHAPTER 8: So Many Niches, So Little Time 65
   From Brainstorm to Bankroll—Pick Your Winning Niche 65
   Exercise #7: Rate and Rank Them All 👥 🔬 66
   Exercise #8: Create a Bio That Fits Your Niche Persona 👥 🔬 . . . 71

ELEMENT #2: Your Fans 75

CHAPTER 9: Find Your Fans to Fund Your Funny 75
   Fans: Your Funny's Financial Lifeline 76
   Reality Check: No Audience = No Career. 76
   The Power of a Niche Fan Base 76
   Case Study: From Fish Markets to Sold-Out Arenas 77
   Exercise #9: Read the Room 79

CHAPTER 10: Infiltrate Your Niche Audience Online 83
   Engage Your Audience—Without Acting Like You Need Therapy . 83

Exercise #10: Reintroduce Yourself to Your Online Audience 🔌 . . 84

CHAPTER 11: Blueprint Your Breakout—How to Hijack 89
Your Rival's Audience

The Jealousy Trap: A Reality Check 89
Case Study: Riding Coattails Like a Pro. 90
Learn From—Don't Copy—Your Competition. 91
Exercise #11: Find Your Blueprint to Success 🔌 91

CHAPTER 12: Post. Bomb. Repeat: The Social Media Strategy . . .99
for Comics Who Want to Get Paid

Why Social Media is the New Comedy Club 99
The Synergy Between Live Shows and Social Media. 100
Success Story: Trevor Wallace—Viral Sensation To 101
Comedy Mogul
Your Platforms: A Comedian's Guide to Owning the 101
Digital Stage
Comedians Who Mastered the Game. 102
Exercise #12: Build Your Social Media Strategy 103
(Without Losing Your Mind) 🔌

ELEMENT #3: YOUR PLATFORM 107

CHAPTER 13: Platform-Tailored Content 107

Why "Come See My Show" is Useless (and What to 107
Do Instead)
Understanding Content Formats 108
Exercise #13: Write Material Specific to Your 110
Niche & Platform 👥 🔌
Repurpose Like a Pro: Post Once, Share Everywhere 111

CHAPTER 14: Work the Crowd, Win the Fans 113

Your Followers Are More Than Just Numbers. 113
Digital Crowd Work: Turning Followers Into Fans 114
Exercise #14: Ignite Your Engagement Game 116

CHAPTER 15: Crush It With Analytics 119
   Why Metrics Are Your Secret Weapon 119
   Your Data's Talking—Are You Listening? 120
   Real-Life Example: It's Never Too Late to Score Big. 121
   Data or Die: The Comedian's Guide to Going Viral 122
   Exercise #15: Metrics, Mayhem, and Making It Big 124

ELEMENT #4: YOUR BRAND 127

CHAPTER 16: Your Quirky Brand. 127
   What Makes You Memorable? 127

CHAPTER 17: Mix and Match Your Niches 129
   Case Study: The Truck Driver Tour Guide 129
   Exercise #16: Niche Mashup .131
   Exercise #17: Use AI to Write Your Brand Title, Description, . . .133
   and Merch Ideas

CHAPTER 18: Define, Diversify & Deliver 135
   Diversify Your Delivery to Define Your Brand 135
   Performance Elements to Consider 136
   Case Study: Justin Willman—Comedy Meets Magic 138
   Exercise #18: Your Performance Toolkit 138

CHAPTER 19: Evolve Through Experimentation 141
   The Alchemy of Testing, Tweaking, and Standing Out 141
   Experimenting with Your Quirky Comedy Brand. 142
   Exercise #19: Workshop Your New Brand Elements 142
   The Seinfeld/Larry David Commitment 143
   Alchemy in Action 144
   Exercise #20: Update and Refine Your Brand Description 144
   Exercise #21: Add Your USP .145

ELEMENT #5: MULTIPLE COMEDY REVENUE STREAMS . . 149

CHAPTER 20: Create Multiple Comedy Revenue Streams 149
   For Everyone Who Did the Work—Congratulations 149
   What You've Built So Far 150

CHAPTER 21: Fast Cash Vs. Forever Cash **153**
   Stop Chasing Gigs. Start Owning Sh*t. 153
   Case Study: How I Made 10x More Without 156
   a Publisher
   Case Studies in Ownership-Based Brilliance 157
   Exercise #22: Comedy Income Reality Check 159

CHAPTER 22: Start a Stream, Grow a River. **165**
   Start Small. Build Big. Own Everything 165
   The Law of Comedy Momentum. .166
   The Free to Fee Pipeline. 167
   Exercise #23: Free to Fee Brainstorming 168
   Double Down on What's Already Working 170
   Exercise #24: Turn Your Day Job into a Comedy Gig 171

CHAPTER 23: Produce the Show That Builds Everything **175**
   Your Signature Show Starts Here 175
   What Counts as a Comedy Product? 177
   Why Your Live Show Is Your Most Powerful Product 177
   Case Studies: Comics Who Built It and Sold It 179
   Exercise #25: The Product is YOU! .180
   Workshop Your Show 184
   Book a Venue 184
   Think Outside the Comedy Club 185
   Collaborate and Share Costs 185
   Negotiate with Venues that Already Have an Audience 186
   Match Your Niche to the Perfect Venue. 186
   Exercise #26: Brainstorm Venues 187
   Exercise #27: Book a Venue 188

CHAPTER 24: Becoming the Possibility of You: **191**
The Final Mindset Shift
   Unlock the Future You've Been Pretending Isn't Possible 191
   Your Mindset Is the Gatekeeper 192
   When the Tools Aren't Enough 192

What You Believe Drives What You Do 193
Meet Your Inner Heckler 194
Exercise #28: Roast Your Inner Heckler 194
    Hack Your Brain: The Prompt That Can Rewrite 195
    Your Subconscious for Success
    Exercise #29: Reprogram Your Mind for Success 196
    Exercise #30: Close the Loop with Your Why 196
    Final Word: Step Into the Possibility of You. 197

The Comedian's Hub. *201*
Other Books by Judy Carter *203*
Acknowledgments *205*

Endorsements from the Pros

"I took Judy Carter's comedy workshop and that's where I learned how to write material."
—**Iliza Shlesinger** on PBS Interview

• •

"Judy Carter can show you how to make your sense of humor pay off."
—**Oprah Winfrey** interviewing Judy Carter on her show about her first book, *Standup Comedy: The Book*

• •

"Judy Carter's workshop launched my comedy career!"
—**Sherri Shepherd**

• •

"Judy Carter helps others find their authentic persona and communicate it in a way that makes audiences laugh."
—**Lily Tomlin**

• •

"Judy Carter puts a comedy spin on workplace stress."
—***Wall Street Journal***

• •

"Judy Carter's book, *The Comedy Bible* is a top resource for writing comedy material and understanding joke structure."
—**Joey Diaz** on Joe Rogan's podcast

• •

"Judy Carter puts a comedy spin on workplace stress and shows how to laugh our way out of it."
—***Wall Street Journal***

* * *

"Judy Carter's *The Comedy Bible* is considered a top ten comedy essential."
—***The Washington Post***

* * *

"I started in Judy Carter's comedy workshop and I attribute her book, *The Comedy Bible* as one of my top 5 all time books. So, if you want guidance in comedy— Carter's books are a great place to start."
—**Maz Jobrani**

Preface

Which Comedy Crisis Is Yours?

Are you:

The Stand-Up Road Warrior Who Can't Fill Your Tank?

Your set kills. The crowd loves you. But somehow, you're still sleeping in your car after gigs to save money on hotels—it's time to get yourself a real bed.

The Open-Mic'er Who Only Performs for Other Broke Comics?

You've mastered making comedians laugh at bringer shows. Unfortunately, landlords don't accept "drink tickets" as rent. Let's level up to a bigger stage.

The Improv Whiz Waiting for SNL to Call?

Your characters are brilliant. Your scenes? Unbelievable. But improv isn't income. Waiting for an SNL audition isn't a business plan. Let's talk about turning "Yes, and" into "Yes, and I can pay my bills."

The Multi-Hyphenate Who'd Like to Be Multi-Incomed?

The singer-songwriter, the drag queen-magician, the tap-dancing ventriloquist, the writer-producer—whatever your act, your talent is undeniable. So why is your bank account ghosting you?

The Fallen Star Searching for a Comeback?

You had the TV deal, the late-night set, the comedy special. Then the phone stopped ringing. Good news: It's not over. Let's relaunch you—on your terms.

The Influencer With No Influence?

Your TikToks are fire. Your Reels are tight. Your followers? Well . . . your mom is very supportive. *Likes* don't pay the bills, and algorithms don't guarantee income. Let's turn your content into cash.

The Writer Who Can't Afford a New Computer?

You've got scripts, jokes, maybe even a whole book sitting in your Google Docs, waiting to be seen. But no agent, no deal, no audience. Time to stop waiting and start getting your words in front of the people who matter—especially the ones with checkbooks.

The Funny Senior Who Isn't Ready to Retire?

You've got stories, experience, and a killer sense of humor. What you don't have? A desire to sit in a rocking chair and fade away. Let's turn your wisdom (and wit) into a business—because you're not done yet.

Sound familiar? Perfect. That means this book is for you. Whether you're a standup, a writer, an improv genius, or any other flavor of funny, I'll show you how to turn laughs into a living—and finally get paid what you're worth. The question is: Are you willing to do something different to *achieve financial security for the rest of your life?*

Let's do it!

What If Your Passions Paid?

Think the comedy market is oversaturated, with too many funny people and not enough cash to go around?
Think again.

Here's the punchline: There's a severe *shortage* of funny people who actually get the business side of show business—and a *surplus* of people ready to throw cash at them. No joke.

I've seen firsthand how my students from my Standup Comedy Workshop have gone on to become household names—including **Iliza Shlesinger, Hannah Gadsby, Seth Rogen, Sherri Shepherd,** and **Maz Jobrani**—and many more who have become successful TV producers, showrunners, and network-approved comedy writers.

So why not *you*?

This book is for the comics, creators, entertainers, and writers who want to go beyond "good" and turn their talent into *paychecks* big enough to make their day jobs jealous.

I don't like to brag, but I wrote *The Bible*. Twice.

The Comedy Bible and *The New Comedy Bible* changed lives. This third book is the most important: It's where the laughs meet the loot.

Buckle up. You're about to turn your punchlines into paychecks.

Introduction

Broke Ain't a Joke

• • • • • • • • • • • • •

*"They say, 'Money can't buy happiness.'
But I just want enough money to know that it's true."*
—Lotus Weinstock

• • • • • • • • • • • • •

Hey, have you heard the old joke:

What's the difference between a stand-up comic and a large pizza? A large pizza can feed a family of four.

It's funny (and sad) because, for most comics, it's true—but it doesn't have to be that way. You can be the exception!

If you're reading this, you most likely crave the rush of a standing O even better than the lying down kind. Comedy is in your DNA. You know it. The audience knows it. Unfortunately, your landlord does not care.

Why Are Headlining Comics Sleeping in Their Cars?

The harsh reality is that the entertainment industry is rigged against performers. Comedy clubs, agents, and managers take the lion's share of the profits, leaving many comics scraping by while still working a day job.

The *LA Times* reports that most comics live below the poverty line, and for actors, about 86 percent of SAG-AFTRA members make less than $26,000 a year. For comics in their first three years, after travel expenses, many lose money—sometimes even $5,000 a year.

There are a few writers who make millions, but according to the Writers' Guild of America (WGA), less than half of their members earn any income from writing, and for those who do, the median income is only $27,000 to $40,000 per year.

> Comics don't quit because they aren't funny—they quit because they're broke and exhausted.

Even headliners—yes, the ones crushing it on stage—often blow their earnings just trying to fill the room. Some even sleep in their cars to cover per diems.

It's a brutal system.

You Deserve Better (and It's Possible)

I know the pain of knowing you have talent . . . and hearing nothing but crickets from the industry. I've seen brilliant comics—hilarious, heartfelt, razor-sharp—walk away because they couldn't make rent.

I almost did, too.

After my mom died, I canceled a gig. The producer didn't like that. Revenge apparently being part of his job description, he called every club I worked at and told them if they booked me, he'd ban them from using his celebrity clients. Boom—career sabotage, no gigs, no money.

I gave up. I decided I should get a *real* job. But . . . I had no job skills unless sarcasm and crowd work count.

So I did what any out-of-work comic would do:

I rented a shared office and pretended to go to work. No joke. It was an acting exercise—a little something I call *method unemployment*.

That's when Linda Adelman—a writer in that shared space—asked me to type for her. I did. She suggested I write a book. So I did.

I sent it to 59 agents.

Got rejected 59 times.

Agent #60? Said yes.

Publisher? Random House.

Reader? Oprah Winfrey.

Next thing I know, I'm on her show.

After that, I stopped chasing club gigs. I discovered that the corporate comedy world—and how to make a living by making people laugh—was a good fit.

That's when I made a decision:

I'd stop begging gatekeepers to let me in—and start building my own damn gate.

That's why I'm writing this book. It's my gift to you.

Because here's what I believe:

People who make others laugh are healers—and healers should be paid well.

This world is stressed, divided, and burned out.

Laughter isn't a luxury anymore—it's medicine.

And *you*, my friend, are the pharmacist.

It's time to get paid.

Yes, it takes a mindset shift.

Yes, it takes some seriously unfunny and unglamorous work.

But once you start treating your comedy like a business, not a hobby—things shift. Doors open. Checks get written.

So the next time someone says, "*You can't make a living doing comedy,*" you'll smile and say, "*Watch me.*"

Let's take this journey together.

I've got your back.

Look for these coaching sidebars throughout the book—think of them like your personal comedy coach with a bullhorn, minus the yelling. (Okay, maybe a little yelling.)

Coaching Tip:
You're in the Right Place

Your act is just the starting line—not the finish line. A comedy career is a marathon, not a mic drop.

You're already in the race by picking up this book. Sitting on the couch, wishing for fame? That's not a strategy.

Putting in the miles? That's how it happens. And I'll be here, cheering you on every step of the way.

For Hand-Holding and Marketing Tips—
Get the *Making Money Being Funny* Workbook

Just know—this book is a deep dive into creating a comedy career designed to make you money. It's going to ask a lot from you. Once you've completed this book, you might want to check out my 30-day companion workbook, which breaks this process into daily, doable actions—complete with writing space, AI prompts, and additional marketing tips.

Available in print or via download at **JudyCarter.com**.

Coaching Tip:
Comedy is a Big Tent—Actors, Singers, Improv Performers, Writers—Come on In

I wrote this book for stand-up comics—but if you're a funny actor, singer, improviser, or writer, or even puppeteer, you're still one of us, and the same principles will apply. Throughout the book, I will provide you with specific tips and examples to guide you.

Chapter 1

Monetize Your Funny—
Create like an Artist, Hustle like a CEO

"I'm not a businessman, I'm a business, Man."
—Kevin Hart on *Late Night with Jimmy Fallon*

The Reality Check

This book isn't selling you a fairy tale. It's about cutting through the glitz and hype with a proven formula—a no-nonsense approach to monetizing your talent that actually works. Thinking that one killer set, one viral clip, or one "big break" will magically launch your career is a slot machine mentality.

Here we trade in luck for strategy—and fleeting fame for a sustainable income model.

From Open Mics to Direct Deposits

This book picks up where *The New Comedy Bible* left off. That book taught you how to write and perform material based on your authentic truths. If you've put in the work—grinding at open mics, bombing spectacularly, then finally getting good—hooray! That was the first step.

Now it's time to get paid.

Because great comics get laughs.

But smart comics get direct deposits.

How?

By thinking about their careers as a business.

By creating a product in a niche.

By building something that lasts longer than your last set.

And here's the shift: The journey to making money being funny begins with a mindset change.

Shift Your Mindset: From Gigging Comic to Comedy Entrepreneur

Being a comedy entrepreneur means seeing yourself not just as a performer, but as a product. Your act, your voice, your unique take on the world? That's your intellectual property. And it can be shaped, packaged, and sold—onstage and beyond.

Let's be clear: Stand-up gigs are critical even if you're a writer. They're your creative lab. They help you sharpen your material, test your brand, and connect directly with your audience. But if you stop there, you're leaving money on the table.

Your goal is bigger than just booking the next gig. It's about creating something that earns money while you sleep.

Sound ambitious? It should.

Sound impossible? It's not.

Let's take a look at someone who's done precisely that.

The Kevin Hart Playbook: From Gig Worker to Mogul

Before selling out arenas, Kevin Hart's day job was selling sneakers. You might assume that performing is his primary income source—but Hart transformed his stand-up career into a multimillion-dollar empire with over 10+ income streams:

- Stand-Up: Arena tours.
- Acting: Movies, TV, commercials.
- Producing: HartBeat Productions.
- Hosting: Talk shows, exclusive content.
- Merch: Tour swag, apparel, and beyond.
- Books: Bestsellers like *I Can't Make This Up*.
- Social Media: Sponsored posts, brand deals.
- Streaming: Netflix specials, partnerships.
- Speaking Gigs: Corporate events that pay big.
- Endorsements: Brands like Nike—yep, still selling shoes, but now for millions. Sort of making money in his sleep. The idea is not to quit what you do, but to expand it.

Hart's brilliance isn't just about being funny—it's about treating his comedy like a business. He didn't just build a fan base—he built a brand. And he gave new comedians the blueprint when he was interviewed on *60 Minutes*:

"I'm no longer just a comedian—I'm an investment, I'm a studio, I'm a partner, looking for partnerships. Work-for-hire is not in my best interest."

Now, maybe you're thinking, "*Well, that's great for Kevin freakin' Hart. But I'm just trying to get five minutes at an open mic without bombing. Netflix isn't exactly calling.*"

And hey, I get it. Right now, all this talk of merchandise, Netflix specials, and multiple income streams might feel like trying to do calculus when you're still figuring out how to hold the pencil. But don't worry—*you don't have to be Kevin Hart to think like a business.*

This book is going to take you step-by-step through what I call Carter's Comedy Cash Formula™—my proven method to turn your funny into a brand, a product, and multiple revenue streams, even if you're starting with nothing but a notebook full of jokes and the courage to get on stage.

Some of you might be thinking, "*So, Judy, if that's true, how come you don't have millions of followers and are selling out arenas?*"

Let's get honest.

── Chapter 2 ──

Why the Hell Should You Listen to Me?

• • • • • • • • • • • •

*"I peaked in junior high.
That was the high point of my life."*
—Larry David

• • • • • • • • • • • •

If I Can Make Money Being Funny, Trust Me—You Can Too

I'm not a household name. Some years, people recognize me on the street. In other years, I could rob a bank in broad daylight, and no one would bat an eye. I don't have a sex tape (yet), and I'm definitely not at my goal weight (you know, what it says on my driver's license).

But here's why you should listen to me: *I'm living proof you don't need a million followers to make real money in comedy.*

Except for one brief, ill-advised stint as a high school drama teacher (where I discovered my primal hatred of teenagers), I've made the bulk of my living from comedy—performing, teaching, writing, and speaking. I've made enough to own a $4 million home in Venice Beach, fly business class to Caribbean scuba vacations, and order appetizers without checking if there's a Groupon.

Right now, I'm writing this book from a beach in Playa del Carmen, sipping a piña colada. (Waiter, make that two!) This isn't bragging—it's proof of what's possible.

And the best part? I still get gigs *on my terms*. I don't have to work anymore. I just want to. I still love working. Do I have Kevin Hart's private jet? No. Do I have Seinfeld money? Also no. However, I do have what I call *freedom money*—the kind of financial security that allows me to say "no" to gigs I don't want and "hell yes" to the ones I do.

You could argue I got lucky, starting before comedy became more crowded than a Trader Joe's parking lot. Fair. But I also fought sexism, ageism, and homophobia. (Those aren't three drag queens I met in Hollywood. They're real obstacles.) Every time I got knocked down, I pivoted, adjusted, and found new ways to make money doing what I love.

Why I'm Telling You This Story

Now, before we dive into the first significant exercise in this book—getting in touch with your "**why**"—I want to share mine with you.

You see, I didn't figure all this out later in life. I started living Carter's Comedy Cash Formula™ before I even knew what it was called.

At the age of ten, I discovered the power of comedy, the hustle of business, and the magic that happens when the two come together. And the exact strategies I used as a kid—niche focus, partnership, promotion, reinvestment—became the foundation of the career (and the income streams) I enjoy today.

This story isn't just a walk down memory lane.

It's here to show you how the seeds of business success can start with a simple "Why."

It's to prove that the formula I'm about to teach you is real, repeatable, and works—whether you're 10 or 70.

How I Became a 10-Year-Old Mogul

At the age of ten, I was a local celebrity. In my Los Angeles neighborhood, I was the go-to magician for children's birthday parties. My journey began when, after getting my tonsils removed, I was rewarded with a magic kit—that had a cover with a photo of a boy with a fake mustache (included in kit) as if it were saying, ONLY DUDES HAVE MAGIC POWERS.

But I had a powerful reason to prove them wrong.

My older sister was disabled. At night, I dreamed of flying her out of her wheelchair like a wizardly superhero. She didn't like magic tricks, so I memorized jokes from my father's book, *Sex Jokes for the John*, and did the next best thing—*I made her laugh*.

Every night at dinner, I'd perform my tricks over and over again, *perfecting my act* for my parents and cracking dirty jokes for my sister. I couldn't make her walk, but I could *levitate her mood*.

One night, my mom's friend caught my act and asked, "How much to perform at my daughter's birthday?" I *negotiated my contract* like a Hollywood agent— $2. My neighbor PeeGee became *my partner,* and just like that—BADA-BOOM—we were in show biz.

Soon, moms from that party were booking us for their own children's events, and suddenly, we had *satellite gigs*! I even printed business cards to *promote* our show and started tracking gigs in a highly sophisticated *client database* (okay, it was a recipe box full of index cards, but still—very official).

I followed up like a pro, secured repeat business. I was a niche *sensation* in West Hollywood.

And when I discovered the *power of money*—and what it could buy that my parents wouldn't (hello, candy and comic books)—I was hooked. But instead of blowing it, I *reinvested* in new tricks, updated my branding, and expanded into charity events and special appearances. I even pitched a story to the *LA Times*—and they published it.

I expanded from birthdays to special events. Now, I was *on the road,* touring foreign places . . . like *The Valley.*

From Birthday Parties to Big-Girl Branding

By the time I was a teenager, I had a *brand*. I leaned into my identity as the only female magician around and created a *quirky feminist edge.* My signature tricks? Escaping from Grandma's girdle and sawing a man in half.

TV producers started calling. I was still a kid, but I had already built a recognizable act in a clearly defined niche—with a message, voice, and a *product*.

That product became a *career*.

I appeared on over 100 TV shows, signed with agents, and even opened for Prince. Yes, *that* Prince.

But success came at a cost. I was on the road 46 weeks a year. My mental health was unraveling, and my bank account wasn't far behind. And as I wrote earlier, after my mom died, I canceled a gig and got banned by a producer. But that actually ended up being a good thing, as it made me do something different:

I *pivoted*.

I wrote a book. Got rejected by 59 agents, and #60 said yes.

Corporations began calling. They wanted me to teach their executives how to use humor. Suddenly, I was a *keynote speaker*. I launched *comedy workshop productions*. And just like that, I had created *multiple income streams*:

- **Standup Gigs**—Landed an exclusive Caesars Palace contract.
- **Teaching**—Launched global careers from my classes.
- **Books**—Published in nine countries, still earning royalties.
- **TED Talks**—Opened the door to high-paying corporate gigs.
- **Coaching**—Helped CEOs and performers get funnier (and richer).

- **Keynote Speaking**—Added a message to my act, quadrupled my fee.
- **Ghostwriting**—TED Talks, joke writing, corporate scripts.
- **TV Punch-Up**—Helped my students sharpen their shows.
- **Merch**—From cassette tapes to online downloads.
- **Memberships**—Built "The Message of You University," generating $200K+ in a year.

I may have started in a shoebox apartment, driving a used Hyundai, but now I own real estate, drive a custom-wrapped electric car, and travel the world—usually on someone else's dime.

And best of all? I've designed a life where the phone still rings with comedy gigs that feed my soul. I get to enjoy my career without the pressure of poverty looming over me.

**Coaching Tip:
You Can Do This**

Overwhelmed? Remember, these income streams started slowly—from birthday parties to teaching comedy in a garage, wondering why I was such a loser. But, over the course of time, I developed business strategies (that I've highlighted in my story) that fueled my success, such as:

- Niche down.
- Know your audience.
- Build your brand.
- Reinvest in yourself.
- Create multiple income streams.

These aren't just childhood flukes. These are the foundational principles I've seen work over and over for comedians who want to turn funny into freedom. However, if reading about my journey makes you feel exhausted or even a little defeated, you're not alone. Maybe you're tired of being broke, but also just . . . tired. I get it. Not everyone wakes up full of motivation, and if you've lost your drive, that doesn't mean you're broken. It means you're human.

Yes, I've had successes, but I've also dealt with insecurity, rejection, and depression. What keeps me going isn't superhuman grit; it's having a *why* that fuels me when nothing else does. That's why I'm not going to throw a mountain at you. This book is designed to break tasks into manageable, achievable steps. And through it all, I will be holding your hand and celebrating your wins to motivate you to keep going.

Coaching Tip:
Motivational Humorists take funny & money to the next level

Sure, corporations sometimes hire stand-ups to do a comedy night at their convention. But here's the truth: The *real* money is in being a funny keynoter with a message. Keynote speakers often get paid *20 times* what they pay comedians—because they're not just entertaining, they're delivering value that aligns with the company's goals. I've made more from one keynote than from two months of headlining clubs. Want to learn how to do it? It's all in my book *The Message of You: Turning Your Life Story into a Speaking Career*.

 **Next Up:** Let's start with the first tool that can help reignite your spark, finding your comedy why.

— Chapter 3 —

Find Your Comedy "Why"

• • • • • • • • • • • • • • • • •

"I always felt like if I could make people laugh, then I had value … it was my way of feeling worthy."
Gary Gulman
(From interviews about his HBO special *The Great Depresh*)

• • • • • • • • • • • • • • • • •

When Comedy Wasn't a Career—It Was Survival

Looking back, I realize my entire career has been guided by one truth I discovered early on: *laughter heals*. It began with my disabled sister. Making her laugh gave me a sense of power over pain. Her laughter showed me that humor could cut through suffering and bring light to the darkest places. She became the *why* behind everything I do. Even now, when I step onto a stage or write a book, I imagine her in the audience, laughing. That image fuels me.

Whether I'm performing stand-up, speaking at a corporate event, writing jokes, or delivering a TED Talk, my message is consistent: *humor has the power to elevate, connect, and heal*. I may have started as a magician with a suitcase full of gimmicks, but the real trick—the real magic—was always laughter.

Exercise #1:
Discover Your "Why" (Hint: Fame Isn't One)

Most professional comedians and successful creatives know their "why." It's the fuel that gets them through rejections, bad gigs, algorithm changes, and those "what-am-I-even-doing-with-my-life" moments.

Gary Gulman uses comedy as a lifeline for his mental health. **Tig Notaro** transformed trauma into legendary stand-up. Now it's your turn. Take a moment to write your origin story.

Write about a moment that first connected you to comedy.
- What drew you to it as a kid, a teen, or an adult?
- Who was the first person you made laugh—and what did that feel like?
- Was there a moment you realized that laughter had power?

Describe the impact you want your comedy (or creative work) to have.
- What do you want people to feel after they experience your work?
- What kind of transformation are you offering them—joy, relief, perspective, permission to feel?

Name the core belief that fuels your creativity.
- Is it "laughter heals"?
- "Truth is funny"?
- Or something only you can write?

Don't overthink it—just start writing. Your "why" isn't a slogan. It's a gut-level truth you come back to when things get tough. It's your North Star.

Exercise Wrap-Up: Know Your *Why*, Own Your Path

**Ask AI This:** (Use ChatGPT or whatever AI tool floats your boat)

[*Insert what you've written about your first moment of making people laugh, your description of the impact you want your comedy to have, and the core belief that fuels your creativity*].

From evaluating what I wrote, reduce my core reason for having a career in comedy into one sentence that I could use to keep me motivated and inspired. If you need more information, please ask me to elaborate until you have uncovered my childhood "why" for devoting myself to a comedy career.

If AI doesn't give you something authentic to you, correct it until you have something that feels true. Print out your core "why" and put it where you can see it every day.

NOTE: If you are unsettled about using AI due to privacy concerns, look for services that offer specific privacy-focused options, such as "incognito" modes, "private" sessions, or "do not train" settings. Many leading AI providers have introduced features to prevent your conversations from being used to train future models and it's easy to register for them.

Coaching Tip:
Use your purpose statement to inspire material.

Here are some of the inspiring statements that comics discovered in my workshop:

> "I create comedy to transform pain into joy, offering others the relief and permission to embrace their authenticity through laughter."
> —**Ceci Walken**.

> "I use comedy to tell the truth women aren't supposed to say—so we can feel less anxious, less alone, and more free."
> —**Kimberly Morrison**.

As someone said, "Comedy is tragedy plus time." Your heartbreaks, humiliations, and awkward truths? That's your treasure trove. Turn pain into punchlines—and every laugh becomes proof you've turned suffering into purpose.

> **Need a Comedy Buddy? A workshop?**
>
> Go to judycarter.com to find comedy resources.

Exercise #2:
From Dream to Game Plan—Create Your Comedy Career Vision

Your "why" is your engine. Now let's put a destination on the map.

Close your eyes for a moment (yes, even you scrolling social media while pretending to read this). Imagine it's five years from now and you've absolutely crushed it in comedy.

- Where are you?
    - Onstage at a packed theater with your name on the marquee?
    - Filming a Netflix special with cameras in your face and Spanx you regret wearing?
    - On a movie set where they're actually laughing at the lines *you* wrote?
    - Or maybe you're leading a sold-out workshop, assisting others to turn their mess into punchlines?
- What does success look like to you—your version, not someone else's?
- Who's in the audience?
    - Strangers who feel like family?
    - Fans wearing your merch?

- ○ Your mom realizing that "open mic" wasn't a phase—it was a launching pad?
- What are you doing that makes you pinch yourself and say, "Holy crap, I can't believe this is my life"?

Write It Down:

Write a vivid description of this future scene. Use details. What do you see, hear, feel, smell (yes, success has a smell—sometimes it's stale beer, sometimes it's a new BMW interior).

Here are some examples from my workshop students:

Example 1: The Stand-Up Headliner

Why:

I do comedy because making people laugh gave me power as a kid when I felt invisible. I believe that humor connects us and makes us feel less alone.

Vision:

It's Saturday night, and I'm standing backstage at a sold-out theater. The house lights dim, and I hear hundreds of people chanting my name. My logo flashes on the screen—merch tables in the lobby are already sold out. I walk onto the stage, and the roar of the crowd hits me like a wave. Every laugh feels electric, like we're all sharing the same heartbeat. My mom's in the front row, crying because she finally "gets it." Netflix cameras are rolling. This is my life.

Example 2: The Writer Turned Showrunner

Why:

I do comedy because writing jokes gave me a voice when I didn't feel heard. I believe that stories—especially funny ones—can shift how people see themselves and the world.

Vision:

I'm walking onto the soundstage where *my* sitcom is being filmed. Actors are rehearsing the words I once scribbled in a coffee-stained notebook. A network exec slaps me on the back: "This show is a hit." Crew members laugh between takes at jokes I wrote. I've got an office full of Emmy swag and a whiteboard covered with ideas for Season 3. My staff writers look to me for guidance, and I recall what it was like when I was in their position. Now, my voice is broadcast into millions of homes every week.

Example 3: The Hybrid Comedian—Speaker

Why:

I do comedy because laughter has healed me during my darkest times, and it can heal others, too.

Vision:

I'm on stage at a healthcare conference in front of 2,000 people. The giant screen behind me flashes my keynote title. Doctors, nurses, and executives are laughing so hard they're wiping tears from their eyes—tears of relief. After my set, people line up to buy my book and take selfies with me. A hospital chain rep pulls me aside to book me for 10 more gigs. Later, I check my phone: my podcast just hit 1 million downloads, and my online course sold another 50 spots overnight. My comedy isn't just making people laugh—it's changing their lives.

Exercise #3:
Turn Your "Why" and "Vision" into Motivation

Ask AI This:

"Based on my comedy 'why' and the vision of success I just wrote, create a motivational vision statement in the present tense. Make it sound like it's already happening, so I can use it as a mantra when I need motivation."

Print your motivational vision statement and put it where you can see it every day. Here is an example:

My comedy connects people through laughter. Every day, I wake up excited to create content that heals stress and brings joy. My shows are sold out, my online clips inspire thousands, and I'm surrounded by creative collaborators who support my success. I'm living proof that being funny is a business—and my humor is making a difference (and making money!).

Next Up: Let's Build Your Game Plan

You've uncovered your *why*. You've pictured your *vision*. Now comes the part where dreams stop being daydreams and start becoming blueprints.

When you know your "why," everything changes. And when you see your vision, it stops being a fantasy and starts feeling possible. You're no longer waiting to be discovered. You're no longer chasing validation. Instead, you're taking ownership of your path.

You're not dipping a toe—you're diving in.

So, if you're ready to stop trading your talent for drink tickets and start building the career you just imagined—turn the page. It's time to build your game plan.

Chapter 4

The Game Plan

"If you don't give up, you can't fail."
—JERRY SEINFELD

How To Use This Book

Sure, talent and a killer set will get you laughs. But if you want to make *money* doing comedy, you need more than a tight five—you need a tight *game plan*.

This chapter lays out your road map to turning laughs into loot, punchlines into profit, and funny into funding your lifestyle. Let's go.

DO THE DEEP DIVES

Each chapter comes with guided brainstorming and tailored exercises to help you uncover the most profitable income streams based on your niche. Want more tools? Workbooks, workshops, and comedy buddies are available at the Comedian's Hub at JudyCarter.com

KEEP YOUR DAY JOB

Newsflash: Keeping your 9-to-5 isn't a failure—it's fuel. Your job gives you a paycheck *and* material. Take a cue from my former student Anne Lippert, who turned working at Home Depot into her first paid gig—for her coworkers! I'll show you how to turn your day job into both stage time and branding gold.

MAKE  AI YOUR SIDEKICK

When you see this icon, it's time to prompt ChatGPT. AI might bomb at writing a solid one-liner, but it's a beast at brainstorming, marketing, lead-finding, and content planning. There is a free version and a paid version. First, create an account that you log into. Then create a "Project: Making Money Being Funny." This way, all of your information will be in one place, and AI can keep track of everything you create. Later in the book, I will ask you to review past exercises, which will help you understand the material more easily. Treat AI like your unpaid intern with zero ego.

> **Coaching Tip:**
> **ChatGPT does lie.**
>
> Although AI is a brilliant writer's assistant, you must remember who is in charge—you! When you receive an answer that doesn't feel right, challenge the AI, ask for a redo, and provide more specific details. The more info you share about yourself, the better the results. AI is a people pleaser. You can ask it to be more critical and/or more practical. In other words, ask for constructive criticism and don't just fall for pretty words.

FIND YOUR ACCOUNTABILITY BUDDY

 This icon? It means: ***Team up.*** You need someone who's just as serious about making this happen. That "hilarious friend who's always high"? Not them. You want a ride-or-die comedy comrade who will call you out when you ghost your goals and celebrate when you land your first paid gig. Visit judycarter.com to find your accountability buddy. Yeah, yeah—someday you'll reach out to someone. How about now in this next exercise?

 ### Exercise #4:
Find Your Accountability Buddy—
The Cure for Procrastination

Procrastinators unite . . . tomorrow. But seriously—accountability is the antidote to inertia. Instead of begging, "I need a partner who can help me do X, Y, and Z," flip it:

Go to judycarter.com and find the link to the "Comedy Buddy" site and post:

> *"I'm the person who shows up on time, nails punchlines, negotiates contracts like a pro, and makes a killer sounding board."*

Boom—you just marketed yourself. The right partner will find you. Bonus: Zoom makes geography irrelevant. Set up a weekly check-in from anywhere in the world.

 **Coaching Tip:**
Invest in Yourself.

Completing just one chapter a week of this book can turn those "impossible" dreams into a seriously profitable reality. It's not about overnight success—it's about building a legacy one step at a time.

Exercise #5:
Seal the Deal—Your Commitment to Comedy (and Yourself)

This is the big kahuna—commitment. No half-assed attempts here. A comedy career demands grit, consistency, and a stubborn refusal to quit—even when your mom suggests law school might be a "safer" bet. Remember what Seinfeld said: "*If you don't give up, you can't fail.*" That's your mantra now.

You're not just dabbling. You're declaring. This is your line in the sand: No quitting. No excuses. Just action.

Write it down, sign it, and let's make it official by sharing with your *Accountability Buddy*:

> I commit to working on this book for at least 15 minutes a day and meeting weekly with my Accountability Buddy. I also commit to *not quitting*, even when it gets hard, scary, or awkward—especially then.

Signed: _____

Sign your commitment online.

Swing by JudyCarter.com to sign your contract online, and I'll be there with motivation—and maybe a bit of friendly peer pressure—to keep you on track.

 **Next Up:** The game-changing formula.

—— Chapter 5 ——

Carter's Comedy Cash Formula™

• • • • • • • • • • • •

"Show business is 80 percent business, 20 percent show. If you don't handle your business, you'll never get the chance to show what you can do."
—Aziz Ansari

• • • • • • • • • • • •

The Math Behind the Laughs—And Why It Pays to Know It

A formula? Judy! I'm a comedian, not a mathematician!

Well, as my grandmother would say, "Try it! You'll like it!"

In *The New Comedy Bible,* my joke-writing formula has helped thousands of comics transform personal problems into punchlines that are guaranteed to kill. It's been used around the world in eight languages—and now we're bringing that same structure to your bank account.

Let's be real: Money messes with your head. One look at your checking balance and you're spiraling—taking dumb gigs, underpricing your value, or ghosting that email from a booker because you *think* you're not ready. But with a clear, rules-based system, you take emotion *out* of your decisions and put power *into* your comedy career.

Think of it as money therapy—with punchlines.

So, drum roll please—here it is:

Carter's Comedy Cash Formula™

Niche + Fans + Platforms + Quirky Comedy Brand = Multiple Revenue Streams

Let's Break the Five Elements Down

NICHE: *What* You Joke About

A comedian without a niche is like a restaurant that serves sushi, BBQ, breakfast, and vegan lasagna. It might be edible, but no one's coming back. Your niche not only makes you stand out but also makes you the go-to comedian for a community that is hungry for material about them.

FANS: *Who* Buys What You're Selling

Your audience isn't just who laughs—it's who follows, clicks, buys merch, and tells their friends. When your audience feels seen, they stick with you for the long haul. Fan loyalty is the engine behind comedy income. Don't have any? I'll show you how to get them.

PLATFORMS: *Where* You're Found

You don't need a big-shot agent to discover you anymore. Your social media platforms are your direct pipelines to fans. You're the media empire now.

QUIRKY BRAND: *Why* You Stand Out

This is your WTF factor. Are you the Tupperware-selling, storytelling drag queen doing a solo show? The hilarious singer who tells her life story through songs while folding her clothes, performing in a laundromat? The funny plumber who gives DIY tips on social media and sells "no crack showing underwear?" Your quirky brand is the magic glue that makes you *one of a kind*.

MULTIPLE REVENUE STREAMS: *How* You Turn Laughs into a Living

Multiple revenue streams are the endgame, as comedy isn't just one-night gigs and tips in a hat. A smart comic thinks beyond the stage—merch, speaking gigs, Patreon subscriptions, books, streaming, and more. This formula builds the ecosystem that feeds your financial future.

 **Next Up:** Personalize the Formula for YOU

Let's start plugging *your* life into this formula. Get ready to rethink how you write, post, and perform—and begin building a career that pays by working Element #1: Finding Your Niche.

ELEMENT #1: YOUR NICHE

— Chapter 6 —

Go Niche Yourself

• • • • • • • • • • • • •

*"I practice ophthalmology by day,
and I practice sarcasm by night."*
—Dr. Will Flanary,
AN OPHTHALMOLOGIST & COMEDIAN WHO BECAME
A VIRAL SENSATION BY SATIRIZING THE MEDICAL WORLD

• • • • • • • • • • • • •

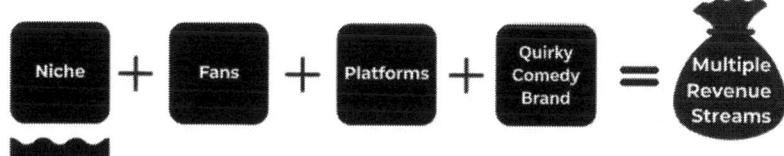

The Math Behind the Laughs—And Why It Pays to Know It

Go niche myself? What if I don't want to, Judy? What does that even mean?

It means doubling down on a specific topic that has a strong following. That topic could be based on your day job, ethnicity, or even your religion. What might help convince you is to know that some of today's wealthiest comics are those you've never heard of—*niche sensations thriving on multiple income streams.*

Ever hear of comedian **Nurse Blake**? If you're in the nursing world, you probably follow him on social media, have seen him live, or bought his custom scrubs. As of this writing, he's on a 35-week stand-up tour selling out 1,500-seat theaters, has his own merch line and magazine, and is signed to a major agency. At 28, he's worth $12 million. Not bad for a guy who jokes about bedpans.

Then there's **Zarna Garg**, a comedian, screenwriter, and full-time Indian immigrant mom who went viral with her YouTube video "What if your kids don't want to marry an Indian?" Over 12 million views later, she's doing sold-out tours, acting gigs, and Amazon specials. Her script won Best Comedy Feature at the Austin Film Festival, and she's currently worth over $2 million—all by *doubling down* on her niche.

And **Tim Hawkins**? He's a Christian comedian with over 150 million YouTube views. His clean comedy fills megachurches, earning $50K–$100K per gig and generating substantial revenue from merchandise and advertising. Current net worth? $2.31 billion. Yes. *Billion*. Praise the Lord and pass the punchlines.

> The riches are in the niches—and broke comics are in "I tell jokes for everybody."

Have I got your attention? Still think "niche" sounds limiting?

The Big Lie: Fame = Fortune

Fame may seem shiny, but it rarely lasts long and can often be a financial drain. Agents, managers, stylists, publicists—they all get paid before you do. Fame is a hamster wheel of exposure without guaranteed income. The entertainment industry can feel like a rigged slot machine: You keep pulling the lever, hoping for a jackpot, while the house wins. There is another way to play this game that can help you win.

The Real Goal: Become a Niche Sensation

Not everyone's destined for Netflix or Madison Square Garden. However, carving out a niche can realistically bring you $300,000 a year or more—and without needing to beg for mainstream approval.

In a world of over 100,000 stand-up comics, blending in is the fastest way to disappear. Your niche is your superpower. It's what makes you memorable, marketable, and monetizable.

Sure, the comedy scene is packed, but how many comics are cracking jokes about Iranian heritage, tech burnout, or being a stay-at-home dad with a Costco obsession? (Now that crowd buys tickets—and snacks in bulk.)

> **Don't Chase the Crowd. Cultivate the Cult.**
>
> You don't need everyone to love you. Just 1% of the U.S.—that's 3.9 million people. Do the math. Sell them a $35 ticket and $40 worth of merch, and you've got a multimillion-dollar comedy business.

Audiences may not remember every joke—they remember you. The hilarious teacher. The comic with ADHD. The ex-Mormon drag queen.

My former student, Vicki Barbolak, turned her trailer park upbringing into a Vegas residency. Look up "Trailer Nasty" comedy—that's her, sipping champagne from a pink double-wide parked on her swanky estate.

Without a niche, you're just another funny person in a sea of open mic hopefuls. Another gal with PMS jokes. Another guy with tired dick jokes. But a niche comic? That's someone people pay to see.

"Old habits don't make new money."
—JUDY CARTER

Coaching Tip:

Playing It Safe = Staying Broke

I'm going to ask you to do something that might be scary—something different.

"If you always do what you've always done, you'll always get what you've always got."

—ANONYMOUS
(BUT PROBABLY SOMEONE IN THERAPY)

Here's the truth—if your current comedy career isn't paying the bills, maybe it's time to rethink it. Take a page from George Carlin:

"I knew I had to change or die creatively."

—GEORGE CARLIN

He reinvented himself from a squeaky-clean image to a cultural icon. You can too. Reinvention isn't risky—stagnation is. Are you willing to take that leap?

There's always that comic—let's call him Mike. He came to my workshop, nodded politely when I suggested creating new material, and went back to bombing with the same stale material. I wrote him a killer set about his supermarket job at the supermarket. He ignored it. Guess who's still stocking shelves? Meanwhile, I got $20,000 to be the funny keynote speaker at a supermarket convention—poetic justice, with a paycheck.

"Trying something new is scary. You know what's scarier? Never evolving."

—JUDY CARTER

WHAT IS AND ISN'T A NICHE?

A niche is less about *you* and more about *them*.

- [X] *Not a Niche*: "I'm a keynote speaker."
- ☑ *Real Niche*: "I'm a keynote speaker who talks to nurses about stress management."
- 💬 Because "I speak to everyone" usually means no one's listening.

- [X] *Not a Niche*: "Clean comedy" or "raunchy comedy."
- ☑ *Real Niche*: "Clean comedy for Christian moms" or "Raunchy comedy about dating after divorce."
- 💬 "Clean" is a style. "Christian mom who teaches Sunday school"—now you've got a fan club.

 **Next Up:** Let's explore your life to mine your niches.

ELEMENT #1: YOUR NICHE

— Chapter 7 —

Comic Undercover: Go Deep to Find Your Niche

• • • • • • • • • • • •

"Comedians are just detectives ... except instead of solving crimes we expose our own dysfunction."
—N<small>IKKI</small> G<small>LASER</small>

• • • • • • • • • • • •

The Comic FBI File—Your Funny Background Investigation

We're about to launch an FBI—a Funny Background Investigation. We're going to dig through your life for that golden thread that makes you YOU. I'll guide you through exploring various niches until we find the perfect fit.

We'll explore niches based on:

- **Who You Are**—Ethnicity, beliefs, mental health, quirks
- **What You Do**—Jobs, hobbies, obsessions
- **Where You Live**—Rural, urban, in a van down by the river?
- **When You Were Born**—Your generation's flavor of chaos
- **Why You Exist**—Upbringing, backstory, whatever made you weird

By the end, you'll have a niche that fills seats, builds a fanbase, and fattens your bank account. You'll stop chasing gigs and start attracting them. You'll go from overlooked to in demand . . . until it's time to swim in even bigger ones.

In this next exercise, you're going to explore a wide range of comedy niches—ones that are *proven to lead to paid gigs*. These aren't just topics; they're targeted pathways to real audiences and *real money*.

A niche isn't just what you joke about—*it's who you're talking to.* You can be a healthcare comic and still talk about your cat or your dating life. But if healthcare is your niche, that's where your gigs come from, where your followers are, and where your marketing dollars go.

Read through the list of niches and note which ones you'll consider building a career around. So, how do you know if a niche is right for you?

As you read through the possible 11 niches in this exercise, ask yourself these five questions:

1. Do you qualify?

You don't get to claim "nurse comedy" just because you once dated a nurse. And a drunken one-nighter doesn't make you LGBTQ+. Your niche must be rooted in lived experience and authentic connection.

2. Do you already have material in this niche?

If you say you're a "teacher comic" but haven't written a single classroom joke—guess what? That's *not* your niche (well, maybe not yet).

3. Are you willing to be an influencer in this niche?

Your posts, your merch, your reels—they'll all need to reflect this niche. If you're not willing to consistently speak to this audience, it's not your niche.

4. Are you surrounded by people in this world?

Your niche should reflect your actual life. If you're doing material about being a boomer, but all your friends are 25-year-old TikTokers (but enough about my life), there's a disconnect. Live the life you're joking about.

5. Does this niche connect to your "why"?

Your niche should line up with the reason you started comedy in the first place. Your pain, your past, your passion—that's what makes your comedy authentic and relatable.

Coaching Tip:

Stick to the Niches I'm Recommending (Seriously)

The niches listed in the upcoming exercises aren't just pulled out of a hat—they've been field-tested with real comedians and vetted for actual, *bankable opportunities*. When I've run this exercise in workshops, some comics went rogue and picked niches like "pigeon rescue," "being unemployed," and the ever-popular but vague "clean comedy." Spoiler alert: those folks are still waiting for a paycheck.

Here's the thing—your niche has to attract a *paying* audience. Unemployed people aren't exactly shelling out for tickets. "Clean comedy" isn't a niche—it's a style that needs to be attached to a *marketable niche*. And as for pigeon rescue? Unless pigeons start hosting corporate retreats, you might want to rethink that. Later in these exercises, you will expand your niche and mix things up, but for now, stick to the list. Your rent will thank you.

Exercise #6:
Find Your Money-Making Niche

Here is your menu of 11 niches:

1. Job
2. Religion
3. Ethnicity
4. Orientation and Gender
5. Mental Health
6. Addiction
7. Disability and Illness
8. Hobbies and Sports
9. Geography
10. Life Stage
11. Commentary and politics

In this exercise, let's explore each of these niches one at a time. At the end of this exercise, you might consider all eleven of them as potentials. That's okay; it's good to have options. In the next exercise, we will narrow them down further.

1. Your Day Job = Your Possible Comedy Goldmine

> *"I took my students to a career fair . . . and started filling out applications myself."*
> —ANDREA CASPARI, TEACHER/COMIC

Before you write off this niche because you hate your job, hold up. That soul-sucking gig? Comedy gold mine. Boss from hell? Fish-microwaving coworker? Boom—material. Work-life comedy *kills* at conferences, corporate gigs, and online. If your job requires a uniform or a punch clock, congrats—you've already got a niche. And a popular one!

> **Success Story: Kenny Brooks @FunnySalesGuy**
>
> **Kenny Brooks** was working as a door-to-door salesman pushing Pink Miracle Shoe Cleaner and doing open mics at night. But everything changed when he reframed his job as a *door-to-door comedian*. First of all, the guy is hilarious, using humor to pitch his product at strangers' front doors. One day, someone filmed him in action. That clip went viral, earning over 300 million views and $800,000 in ad revenue.
>
> He rebranded as @**FunnySalesGuy**, signed a Netflix deal, and was invited to speak at a **Tony Robbins** event, as you guessed it—a funny sales guy. And get this—he still keeps his sales job because it continues to fuel his YouTube revenues, merchandise sales, commissions, and licensing deals, not to mention being the top salesman for the Pink Miracle Shoe Cleaner Company.
>
> *Moral of the story?* What you do for a living may be the secret to your success, hiding in plain sight.

Success Stories:

Andrea Caspari—High School Teacher
From classroom chaos to the Bored Teachers Comedy Tour, performing for thousands, and now earning a living from comedy.

Alonzo Bodden—Aircraft Mechanic
Parlayed his blue-collar background into a win on Last Comic Standing, multiple specials, and steady touring.

Corey Rodrigues—Salesman-Turned-Comic
Turned his work in sales and corporate training into comedy and now does standup, corporate gigs, cruise ships, and dry bar comedy.

Consider your day job as a niche by answering these questions:
1. Do you qualify?
2. Do you already have material in this niche?
3. Are you willing to be an influencer in this niche?
4. Are you surrounded by people in this world?
5. Does this niche connect to your "why"?

If the answer to these *five* questions is "yes," it could be time to *turn your day job into a comedy career.*

Ask AI This: Your Day Job as a Niche

Prompt: How can I use my expertise in [INSERT YOUR DAY JOB] as a comedy niche to gather followers and make money? Please list any comedy spin-off possibilities.

> **EXERCISE RESULTS:**
> **IS YOUR OCCUPATION YOUR MONEY-MAKING NICHE?**
> ☐ YES
> ☐ NO
> ☐ MAYBE

2. RELIGION NICHE

"Next Sunday, we'll be having a bake sale to raise money for the youth mission trip. Jesus died for your sins, but Karen's cookies are $1 each."

MICHAEL JR., CHRISTIAN COMIC

Faith-Based Funny Can Fill Seats (and Your Bank Account)

Religious material isn't just a gold mine for jokes—it's a real business opportunity. If your act leans towards clean or spiritually themed content, faith-based gigs can be incredibly lucrative. From megachurches and Muslim festivals to synagogue fundraisers and interfaith conferences, religious spaces book comics—and pay well.

Success Stories:

Chonda Pierce—*Christian Niche*
One of the top Christian comedians in the world, earning between $20,000–$50,000 per show, performing at women's conferences, megachurches, and faith-based events with audiences of 10,000+.

Alex Edelman—*Jewish Niche*
Created *Just For Us*, a solo show about identity, faith, and white nationalism—won a Peabody, a Tony, and a Netflix special.

Coaching Tip:
Religion as a Niche

Not every religion is a comedy cash cow. Sure, atheist jokes can kill on stage—but good luck booking a tour of atheist conventions with a merch table full of nothing. That said, many religious communities do pay—and pay well. For the right comic with the right message, your money can be fruitful . . . and multiply.

Azhar Usman—*Muslim Niche*
Toured globally with *Allah Made Me Funny*, blending faith and stand-up comedy.

**Coaching Tip:
Writing Material for Religion**

Right now (yes, now), scan the next 30 days in your calendar. Anytime you've got a religious event—church service, temple gathering, prayer group, kids' choir—block off 30 minutes immediately afterward for writing. Use those fresh impressions to generate material while it's still buzzing in your head.

If you haven't set foot in a religious space in years? Or if you are a comic and do not have one joke about growing up in a religion, that's your sign to skip this niche and move on to the next one.

**⊙ EXERCISE RESULTS:
IS RELIGION YOUR
MONEY-MAKING NICHE?**
☐ YES
☐ NO
☐ MAYBE

3. ETHNICITY AS YOUR NICHE

"My mom made spaghetti . . . Filipino spaghetti. She put hot dogs in it."
—Jo Koy

Your Culture = Your Comedy Superpower

Ethnicity is more than background—it's a brand. Comedy rooted in cultural identity creates instant relatability and tremendous opportunities. Whether you're first-gen, an immigrant, or grew up between two cultures, there's an audience hungry for your truth (and your impressions of your mom).

Success Stories:

Hasan Minhaj—South Asian-American
Launched *Patriot Act*, won Peabody Awards, and pulled in $75K–$150K per appearance—net worth: over $12 million.

Ali Wong—Asian-American
Turned her immigrant family experience into Netflix hits *Baby Cobra* and *Hard Knock Wife*, launching her into superstardom.

Jo Koy—Filipino-American
His family-based comedy sells out arenas worldwide, leading to Netflix specials and a movie deal—with an estimated net worth of $5 million or more.

When Your Ethnicity Gets You in the Writers' Room

Writers also need to niche themselves in today's TV landscape; authenticity matters. When studios greenlight a show about a specific cultural community, they often seek writers *from* that community to get the tone right. That means your background isn't baggage—it's your golden ticket.

Black-American?
Quinta Brunson created the Emmy Award-winning *Abbott Elementary* TV series not just as a workplace sitcom, but as a love letter to Black teachers and underfunded public schools. The show's success isn't just about great jokes—it's about hiring writers who lived the experience. Brunson built a team of comedy writers with deep roots in Black culture, ensuring every line feels like the show was lifted from a real classroom in Philly.

Korean-American?
Beef creator **Lee Sung Jin** didn't just write a rage-fueled dramedy—he pulled together a writers' room filled with Asian-American

voices who understood the quiet pressure of immigrant families and the loud chaos of repressed anger. The result? A show that swings between dark laughs and cultural truth bombs, all grounded in the specificity of the Korean-American experience.

Mexican-American?

Linda Yvette Chávez, co-creator of Netflix's *Gentefied*, was hired specifically because she could bring the authentic East L.A. Mexican-American voice to the screen. Her background wasn't just relevant—it was required.

South Asian-American?

Mindy Kaling got her start writing for *The Office*, but it was her Indian-American identity that powered *The Mindy Project*, *Never Have I Ever*, and *Velma*. These shows needed a writer who knew what it was like to grow up brown, funny, and complicated.

> "The more specific I got, the more universal it became."
>
> —MINDY KALING

**Coaching Tip:
Hybrid Yourself**

Some identity-based niches—like Asian, African American, Latinx, Middle Eastern/North African, American Indian/Alaskan Native, and Native Hawaiian/Pacific Islander—are still underrepresented on Netflix and beyond. That means there's space to stand out.

But if you find that your niche is already crowded (looking at you, "white guy with a podcast"), consider *hybriding* yourself. Combine your background with an emerging niche—like "Gay African American," or "Asian American with Bipolar Disorder." The more specific and authentic you are, the more you cut through the noise. In comedy, intersectionality isn't just a buzzword—it's a brand strategy.

Coaching Tip:
Ask yourself the five questions for niche consideration

Confused about whether something is your niche? Don't forget to ask yourself the five questions on page 42.

EXERCISE RESULTS:
IS YOUR ETHNICITY YOUR MONEY-MAKING NICHE?
- [ ] YES
- [ ] NO
- [ ] MAYBE

4. ORIENTATION & GENDER

"I didn't come out until I was 25. I thought I was straight. I just hadn't met a guy I wanted to kiss . . . or touch . . . or look at."
—**Fortune Feimster**

Own Your Truth, Build Your Audience

Whether you're LGBTQ+ or a straight woman connecting with a queer fanbase, this niche is all about radical authenticity. Queer comics and women who speak truthfully about gender roles build loyal, loving audiences—and that loyalty pays off.

> Your truth is your clickbait—and in this case, clickbait pays.

Success Stories:

Cameron Esposito—Lesbian, Catholic
Her stand-up special, *Rape Jokes*, raised funds for survivors and solidified her brand across podcasts, TV, and books.

Fortune Feimster—Lesbian Comic
From *Chelsea Lately* to *Netflix*, Fortune has built a fan base around body positivity and same-sex love.

Trixie Mattel and Katya Zamolodchikova—Drag Queens
Trixie and Katya turned their drag personas into multimillion-dollar empires through touring, podcasts, YouTube, books, and even a cosmetics line.

```
⊙ EXERCISE RESULTS:
IS ORIENTATION & GENDER
      YOUR NICHE?
   ☐ YES
   ☐ NO
   ☐ MAYBE
```

5. MENTAL HEALTH AS YOUR NICHE

> *"Depression is like a bad roommate. It eats your food and never cleans up."*
> —MARIA BAMFORD

Comedy That Connects—and Heals

Anxiety, depression, OCD, BPD—what used to be taboo is now your ticket to empathy-based comedy that hits hard and pays well.

> If you can joke about your panic attack without having one, you've got material.

Success Stories:

Maria Bamford—Bipolar, OCD
Built a career around mental illness, with Netflix specials, a semi-autobiographical sitcom, and book deals.

Taylor Tomlinson—Anxiety, Bipolar
Look at You and *Quarter-Life Crisis* made her a Netflix star, with multimillion-dollar tours.

Connor DeWolfe—ADHD with LOLs
Connor DeWolfe turned his neurodivergent brain into a social media gold mine, building a massive following with fast-paced, hilarious skits about living with ADHD. His hyper-relatable content, quirky characters, and rapid editing style landed him brand deals, Patreon fans, and merch sales—making his brain fog bankable.

Ask AI This: Is my mental health a good money-making niche?

Prompt: I'm considering my mental health as a money-making niche. My condition is: [INSERT YOUR CONDITION]. Please let me know by searching hashtags on popular social media if this is a topic that can generate clicks and revenue, and if there is funny content geared towards that audience.

EXERCISE RESULTS:
IS MENTAL HEALTH YOUR MONEY-MAKING NICHE?
- [ ] YES
- [ ] NO
- [ ] MAYBE

6. ADDICTION NICHES

"I told my therapist I was addicted to porn. She said, 'Let's unpack this.' I said, 'That's the problem—I can't stop unpacking it.'"
—NEAL BRENNAN

From Rock Bottom to Netflix Special

Whether it's drugs, gambling, video games, or doom scrolling—addiction turns pain into punchlines. The key? Turn your recovery (or relapse) into relatable comedy.

> If they can't look away, they'll pay to look— and laugh.

Success Stories:

John Mulaney—Coke Addiction
His special, *Baby J*, chronicled his relapse and rehab and landed him a fresh Netflix deal worth millions.

Craig Conant—Sober Comic
Turned his recovery into a viral brand and regularly tours with comedy giants like Bill Burr.

Ron Funches—Gaming Addiction Comic
Addicted to gaming? Ron provides hilarious commentary on Twitch while streaming games like *Overwatch* and *WWE 2K*, earning money from subscriptions, Twitch ad revenue, game collaborations, and Patreon.

```
┌─────────────────────────────────┐
│  ⊙ EXERCISE RESULTS:            │
│    ARE ADDICTIONS YOUR          │
│    MONEY-MAKING NICHE?          │
│    ☐ YES                        │
│    ☐ NO                         │
│    ☐ MAYBE                      │
└─────────────────────────────────┘
```

7. DISABILITY & ILLNESS NICHE

> *"Dating is hard when you have a disability. What's my type? Someone with low standards."*
>
> —R**YAN** N**IEMILLER**

Your Disability Could Be Your Booking Agent

If you have a condition, illness, or difference that makes people uncomfortable—congratulations, you have a niche. These comics don't shy away from their diagnosis; they lean into it and cash in on it.

Success Stories:

Maysoon Zayid—Cerebral Palsy

TED Talk star, actress, and global touring comic who blends disability and identity for packed houses.

Ryan Niemiller—Congenital Disability

A finalist on *America's Got Talent*, Ryan turned his limb difference into a high-profile, blue-collar act.

Tig Notaro—Cancer Survivor

Her "I have cancer" set became a Grammy-nominated album and a Netflix special as her career took off post-mastectomy.

Ask AI This: Does your disability have a following and gigs?

I'm [INSERT YOUR DISABILITY] and considering it as my comedy niche. Please let me know about organizations, both online and in-person, that would be interested in sponsoring comedy about my specific disability.

EXERCISE RESULTS:
IS DISABILITY & ILLNESS YOUR MONEY-MAKING NICHE?
- ☐ YES
- ☐ NO
- ☐ MAYBE

8. HOBBIES AND SPORTS NICHE

> *"People are surprised when I say I'm into pottery. They expect me to be more into smoking bowls than making them."*
>
> —SETH ROGEN

Turn Your Passion Into Your Paycheck

From baking pies to Pokémon, from hunting to Pickleball, your weird little hobby or your success in sports could become a comedy niche that builds a loyal following. Fans love comedians who share their passions—especially when they're oddly specific and can become an online niche sensation, creating ad revenue and merch.

Success Stories:

Seth Rogen—Pottery & Pot
Turned his ceramic obsession into a luxury ashtray business, a TV show, and a cannabis brand worth millions.

Andrew Rea—Cooking with Comedy

Andrew Rea didn't stick to the stage—he turned his love of food into *Binging with Babish*, a YouTube empire blending comedy and cooking. With humor as his secret ingredient, he has built a multimedia brand featuring cookbooks, branded merchandise, and a massive online following.

Charles Phoenix—Nostalgia Collector

Built a solo show retro slideshow, leading to books, merch, and a national fanbase obsessed with mid-century kitsch.

Kelsey Cook—The Foosball Comic

Kelsey Cook turned an unlikely side hustle—professional foosball—into a comedic goldmine. Blending her sharp wit with her killer hand-eye coordination, she launched *Wrists of Fury*, a YouTube series where she interviews comedians while demolishing them at the table. Her one-of-a-kind brand catapulted her to touring headliner status, TV spots, a hit podcast, and a merch line that proves comedy (and foosball) are all in the wrist.

> **◉ EXERCISE RESULTS:**
> **ARE HOBBIES & SPORTS YOUR MONEY-MAKING NICHES?**
> ☐ YES
> ☐ NO
> ☐ MAYBE

Is your hobby or sport a niche? Yes, no, maybe.

9. GEOGRAPHY NICHE

> *"Living in New York is like dating a narcissist. It treats you like trash, but when it loves you—you're hooked again."*
>
> —MICHELLE WOLF

Where You're From = Who Gets You

Your hometown, accent, or regional quirks can become your signature. Whether you're a New York neurotic or a Midwest nice-guy, geography gives your comedy flavor, authenticity, and built-in fans, especially if you are from a small town.

> If your accent is the punchline, congratulations—
> you have a niche.

Success Stories:

Jeff Foxworthy—Georgia Redneck

In the late 1980s, I met a Southern comedian named Jeff Foxworthy at *The Comedy Store* in LA. He had a thick Georgia accent, and New York comics mocked him, calling him a "redneck." Instead of running from the label, he embraced it.

One night in Michigan, performing in a club next to a bowling alley with valet parking (yes, that's a real thing), a heckler called him a redneck. Foxworthy shot back:

> *"Look out the window, for crying out loud. If you've got valet parking at a bowling alley—you might be a redneck."*

The audience erupted. That night, he locked himself in his hotel room and wrote ten more *You Might Be a Redneck* jokes. The rest is comedy history—*The Tonight Show* appearances, a sitcom, the *Blue Collar Comedy Tour*, hosting gigs, more than two dozen books, and a net worth of over $100 million.

Lesson? Lean into your unique background—even if it's covered in mud and chewing tobacco.

Sebastian Maniscalco—Chicago Italian
Built a brand on family and hometown culture, leading to arena tours and a net worth of $35M+.

Shawn Pelofsky—Jewish Cowgirl
Mined her upbringing in Oklahoma for jokes that landed her on cruise ships, tours, and niche shows with cult followings.

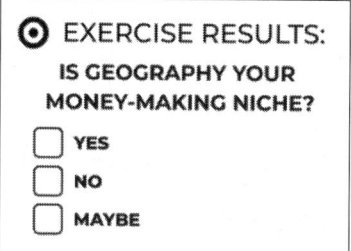

10. LIFE STAGE NICHE

> *"It seems like just yesterday I was taking acid... and now I'm taking antacid."*
> —JUDY CARTER

From Breastfeeding to Bingo
Parenthood, menopause, student debt, retirement—these aren't just stressors, they're content. Your generation's shared pain = your sold-out show.

Coaching Tip:
Life Stage Niches Work Best When They're Marginalized

Your life stage only qualifies as a niche if it's underrepresented in comedy. Boomers? Pregnant women? Menopausal women? Audiences will flock to you because they never see themselves on stage.

Case in point: I once sold out a 1,500-seat theater in Iowa in just 48 hours. Why? Because when was the last time you heard a menopause joke on TV? Exactly—never.

But if you're a young comic? Sorry, you're just like half the other comedians out there. That's not a niche—that's the default setting.

Success Stories:

Carole Montgomery—Women 50+

Creator of *Funny Women of a Certain Age*, four Showtime specials, and a national tour with packed theaters.

Mommy Tonk:
Turning Parenting into a Musical Meltdown

Shannon Noel and Stacie Burrows created *Mommy Tonk*, a musical comedy show centered around the highs and lows of raising kids. Their performances sell out because they tap into experiences mothers find deeply relatable—whether it's sleep deprivation or kids destroying expensive furniture.

Song title: *"If you haven't signed up for summer camp yet, you'd better get your ass in gear."*
—*Mommy Tonk*, the musical comedy show

Nicole Blaine—Breastfeeding Comic

Launched BYOB (Bring Your Own Baby) comedy shows at her own club, monetizing motherhood with mics.

> **EXERCISE RESULTS:**
> **IS YOUR LIFE STAGE YOUR MONEY-MAKING NICHE?**
> ☐ YES
> ☐ NO
> ☐ MAYBE

11. COMMENTARY COMIC NICHE

"As an outsider, I had the advantage of perspective. I wasn't shaped by the same mold so that I could see its cracks."
—TREVOR NOAH

Turn Headlines into Punchlines

If you're already roasting politicians, culture wars, or the Kardashians in your group chat, you might be a commentary comic. This niche thrives online, in podcasts, and anywhere hot takes meet humor.

> If you're already yelling at the news, you might as well get paid for it.

 **Coaching Tip:**
Turn Scrolling into Scripting

For every 30 minutes you spend doomscrolling, invest 10 minutes turning what you just saw into material. Write down three ideas right now for your next reel—before the algorithm eats your attention span..

> ### Commentary Comedians Are in Danger
>
> This niche comes with its own set of risks. In politically volatile regions, making jokes about influential people can have real consequences.
>
> One prominent Indian comedian, **Kunal Kamra**, made a seemingly minor onstage jibe at a right-wing politician in Mumbai. Even without naming names, an angry mob attacked the venue. Kamra is currently under investigation for alleged defamation and remains in hiding. He refused to apologize and took to X to call out the "inability to take a joke at the expense of a powerful public figure."

A reminder: *commentary comedy is powerful—and dangerous*. Choose your battles wisely.

Success Stories:

John Oliver—Political Satirist

Built *Last Week Tonight* into a multi-Emmy-winning platform with global reach.

> ### Shabaz Ali—Commentary Comic Roasting the Rich (and Getting Paid for It)
>
> With 1.9 million TikTok and 1.6 million Instagram followers, Shabaz Ali skewers influencer excess with deadpan reaction videos that call out the ridiculous aspects of wealth and social media culture. His viral success has translated into real revenue, with ad deals, brand sponsorships, merchandise sales, and his hit book, *I'm Rich, You're Poor*, all contributing to his estimated six-figure income. While he's best known for his online content, his growing brand suggests that live shows and events are part of the package as well.

Kathy Griffin—Gossip Queen
Dished on D-listers, earned A-list cash: multiple specials, best-selling memoirs, and a loyal LGBTQ+ audience.

Amber Ruffin—Late Night Maverick
Blends smart social takes with biting jokes that go viral weekly—and helped redefine diversity in late-night comedy.

What Qualifies You for This Niche?
You don't need a political science degree. But you *do* need:
- A deep obsession with the news, celebrity culture, or online discourse.
- Strong opinions (and the ability to turn them into punchlines).
- A love of truth-telling with a twist—even if it ruffles feathers.
- Comfort with being polarizing. Commentary comics aren't for everyone—and that's a *good* thing.

> *"I have an almost obsessive need to process information into comedy. If I didn't, I'd lose my mind."*
> —J‍OHN O‍LIVER

Fans in this niche love a comedian who helps them *laugh so they don't scream.*

EXERCISE RESULTS: IS COMMENTARY & POLITICS YOUR MONEY-MAKING NICHE?
- [ ] YES
- [ ] NO
- [ ] MAYBE

REVIEW: Potential Niche List

Circle all your "yeses" and "maybes":
- Job
- Religion
- Ethnicity
- Orientation and Gender
- Mental Health
- Addiction
- Disability and Illness
- Hobbies and Sports
- Geography
- Life Stage
- Commentary and politics

 **Next Up:** Let's Narrow This Down!

ELEMENT #1: YOUR NICHE

— Chapter 8 —

So Many Niches, So Little Time

• • • • • • • • • • • • •

"I have no idea what my niche is. I'm just hoping it finds me before the rent is due."
—ALI WONG

• • • • • • • • • • • • •

From Brainstorm to Bankroll—Pick Your Winning Niche

Can you believe it? We actually made it through this deep dive into your one-of-a-kind comedic identity. You've dissected your background, your quirks, and those *questionable* career choices—basically, your whole life just got roasted under a comedy microscope.

Now for the fun part: picking the niche (or combo) that'll put your bank account into the red. With this book, your *Accountability Buddy,* and your workbook, you've got more self-awareness than a therapy session—but let's be real, not every funny thought belongs onstage. Some bits are gold; others are just inside jokes with your dog.

Finding your comedy niche is like finding the perfect pair of jeans—when it fits, you can feel it. You've brainstormed, had your lightbulb moments, and now you're staring at a list of ideas longer than a CVS receipt. You can't be everything to everyone. Time to trim the fat, lock in your top three comedy identities, and carve out your corner of funny. Let's do this.

>  **Coaching Tip:**
> **Stick to the Bankable Niches**
>
> Resist the urge to go rogue! A niche that's not on the top 11 list will probably have zero market. Remember, your niche isn't just "a story about me"—it's a magnet that pulls in like-minded people who share a common interest, struggle, or identity. When done right, your niche becomes the club your audience wants to join. And spend money on..

Exercise #7:
Rate and Rank Them All

You've explored a variety of possible niches—identity-based, profession-based, lifestyle, mental health, and more. By now, your notebook (or the margin of this book) should be filled with niche ideas. But before you move forward, it's time to narrow the field. It's best to do this with your Accountability Buddy, as an outside perspective can help narrow the field faster.

> A good niche doesn't just tell your story—it gets your audience saying, "That's my story too."

Let's make your niche work **for you**—financially, creatively, and personally.

Step #1: The Niche Filter: Rate Each Niche From 1 to 5

(1 = Not true at all, 5 = Absolutely true)

Question	Niche #1	Niche #2	Niche #3	Niche #4	Niche #5
I have lived experience in this world.					
I already have jokes or material in this niche.					
I'd feel comfortable being known for this niche.					
My social media presence could reflect this niche.					
I actually live this lifestyle (friends, events, community).					
This niche connects to my "why" for pursuing comedy.					
TOTAL					

Total each column. The highest scores are your most viable options.

Step #2: Choose Your Top Three

Now, based on your scores, select the top three niches that:
- Feel most true to you
- Spark comedic material easily
- Connect you to a clear audience

Main: _____

Secondary: _____

Wildcard (Could evolve later): _____

Step #3: Revenue Possibility Might Help Narrow Down Your Niche

A niche you're only moderately passionate about may have the *most significant potential to elevate your bank account.* That doesn't mean selling out—but it does mean getting smart. *Passion is great. Payment is greater.*

Before doubling down on your niche, ask yourself: *Is anyone actually paying for this kind of comedy?* Because putting your time, creativity, and marketing into something that can't be monetized might be fun—but it won't pay your rent.

Use the AI prompt below to help you commit with both your heart *and* your wallet:

> I live in [INSERT CITY]. Based on my location and [NICHE], evaluate:

1. **Live Show Opportunities**—Beyond comedy clubs, what local or regional money-making gigs (within driving distance) exist for a comedian in this niche? Include:

   - Industry events
   - Corporate gigs
   - Association conferences
   - Fundraisers or community events
   - Colleges or specialty venues
   - Social media revenue
   - Festivals
   - Additionally, any specific organizations that would book a comedian.

2. **Corporate & Keynote Potential**—Could this niche lend itself to paid speaking engagements or keynotes with a comedic angle? Suggest relevant industries or causes.

3. **Merchandising Ideas**—Are there catchphrases, inside jokes, or character ideas that could become merch (shirts, mugs, stickers) appealing to this niche audience?

4. **Online Income Potential**—Evaluate the likelihood of building a substantial online following as a [INSERT NICHE] comedian. Include possible formats (YouTube, TikTok, podcast, blog) and what kind of content might attract sponsors, brand deals, affiliate sales, or digital product income.

5. **Overall Market Viability**—Based on current trends and audience interest, is there a genuine market—live or online—for a comic in this niche? How saturated or underserved is this space?

Let the data help you decide if a niche is not only authentic but also sustainable.

Here are examples of revenue streams based on a geography-based niche that expand beyond just stand-up comedy.

- Local sponsorships, regional tours, themed merch (e.g., "Detroit Hustles Harder" shirts), and YouTube content on city life.
- Small-Town Comedy
- State fairs, niche storytelling shows, and social media content for rural audiences.
- Accents & Regional Slang
- TikTok/YouTube character sketches, voice-over gigs, brand collaborations.
- Speaking gigs for cultural events, comedy specials, and book deals.
- Hometown Nostalgia
- Live storytelling shows, historical tourism collaborations, and comedy specials focused on city pride.

> For example, a comedian from New Orleans could create a food + comedy web series reviewing local restaurants. Revenue streams? Sponsorships from restaurants, tourism board deals, and brand partnerships.

Step #4: Stuck Between a Few Niches? Try a Hybrid!

If two of your top niches feel like they overlap, *merge them* into a strong comedic identity. Later, we will revisit hybrid niches as a way to develop your Quirky Comedy Brand.

Examples:

- "*The Italian Teacher with ADD*"
- "*A Queer Immigrant Dad Navigating Texas*"
- "*A Divorced Millennial Cat Mom Working in Tech*"

Coaching Tip: Niche Mashups

Let's say a niche high on your list is "Life Stage." When you position yourself as an expert on your generation's quirks, struggles, and slang, you tap into a built-in audience that gets it. The key? Combine it with another niche for maximum impact.

Think:
- Millennial with ADHD—juggling avocado toast, anxiety, and impulse buys.
- Gen Z in the Workplace—navigating Zoom calls, side-eyes, and side hustles.
- Boomer Tech Support Survivor—every joke starts with, "So I was on the phone with my dad for two hours..."
- Single Gen X Parent Dating Again—raising teens while ghosting Tinder matches.

Generational humor resonates most deeply when it's personal and painfully relatable.

What are the hybrid niches you can come up with when you combine a few of your top choices?

Your Hybrid Niches:

1. _____

2. _____

3. _____

 **Exercise #8:
Create a Bio That Fits Your Niche Persona**

Step #1: Give Them a Test Run

Now that you have mashups, let's test them out with your Accountability Buddy. Share your top three niches and ask:

- Does this sound like me?
- Is it specific, memorable, and marketable?
- Would this make you want to book me or follow me?

If your buddy gives you a blank stare or says, "That could be anyone," you may need to revisit and refine your niche until it truly reflects who you are and what makes you unique and funny.

Step #2: Craft Your New Bio

Once you've identified your top niche(s), and with support from your Accountability Buddy, it's time to craft your bio—something you can use on your website, social media, pitches, and press releases. This is the new you!

Ask AI This:

Write a short, funny, and impressive bio for a stand-up comedian whose niche is [MAIN NICHE], blending in their background as [REAL-LIFE EXPERIENCE] and [COMEDY EXPERIENCE/BOOKINGS]. Make it authentic, engaging, and Booker-ready to include not only comedy stand-up gigs, but also other revenue streams that are appropriate for this niche.

Example:

Write a short, funny, and impressive bio for a stand-up comedian whose niche is "Queer Teacher with ADHD," blending in their background as a former high school drama teacher and finalist in the Portland Comedy Festival. Make it authentic, engaging, and Booker-ready to include not only comedy stand-up gigs, but also other revenue streams that are appropriate for this niche.

If the result doesn't sound like you, tweak the prompt until you get a bio that feels just right.

Step #3: Go Public

Let's get your bio(s) out there and put them on your website.

Final Thought: Start with Your Niche and Evolve

I know many of us have problems with commitment. Forget about our careers; many of us can't even commit to a mobile phone contract. Just know—this is your starting place. If your niche isn't working, pivot. Comedy (and life) is all about adaptability. But by narrowing your focus now, you're setting yourself up for a successful, profitable comedy career.

> **Remember:** Your niche isn't a limitation. It's your launchpad.

>>> **Next Up:** Build Your Audience

Before you start laughing all the way to the bank, we need to discuss how to turn your niche into multiple comedy revenue streams—starting with building an audience. Let's find your fans.

| ELEMENT #2: YOUR AUDIENCE |

Chapter 9

Find Your Fans to Fund Your Funny

"Find your weirdos. The world is big. If you find your weirdos, they'll support you forever."
—COMEDIAN CHRIS GETHARD

Carter's Comedy Cash Formula™

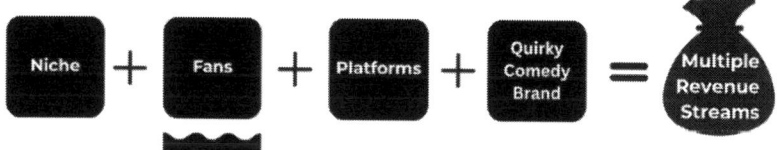

Your Niche + Your Fans/Audience = Comedy Gold

Question: *What is a comedian without a fan base called?*

Answer: *A waiter. (Sorry, not sorry.)*

So, you've found your niche—congrats! That's a huge win. I'm proud of you. You've done the inner work. Now it's time to turn outward.

Because the next element of your *Carter's Comedy Cash Formula*™ isn't about who you are—it's about who's watching. Or more importantly, who should be watching.

Fans: Your Funny's Financial Lifeline

Your fans are the ones who fund your funny. They're the reason you can pay rent, upgrade from instant ramen, and buy a second mic for your podcast (that you swore you'd keep going).

If you've nailed your niche, your fans already have something in common with you—whether it's techies hating buzzwords, helicopter parents pitting oat milk against almond milk, or millennials who think "adulting" should come with a trophy. You're part of their world now, and it's time to invite them into yours.

Now, we double down. You're not just performing at them. You're speaking to them.

Reality Check: No Audience = No Career

Excellent material with no audience is like a phone with no signal:

Sad. Lonely. Unusable.

Your job now? Find the weirdos who want what you've got.

And no, your mom doesn't count (unless she brings 200 people and buys a hoodie).

You need real fans—people who would pay to see you, wear your merch in public, and defend you online when someone says, *"Meh, I don't get her."*

The Power of a Niche Fan Base

Let's get one thing straight:

Numbers matter.

Agents, managers, and brands don't just want to know if you're funny. They want to know if people show up when your name's on the poster.

Your job is to build *that* following.

Not fake followers. Not your cousin's cousin who "likes everything." Real fans. Ride-or-die people who feel like you're telling *their* story. Think of your fan base like a relationship.

They need attention. Engagement. The occasional Instagram flirtation.

Like that houseplant you forgot to water, your fans *will* wilt without love. But if you give them light and attention?

They thrive. And they'll grow with you.

Case Study: From Fish Markets to Sold-Out Arenas

Jo Koy's rise to comedy superstardom is a masterclass in niche marketing. Jo Koy didn't wait for a Netflix deal to start building his audience. He leaned into his roots—Filipino culture, family quirks, and community events. He didn't try to bring his audience to a comedy club—he went to them, performing at fish markets, church functions, fundraisers—anywhere his community gathered.

Then he took a bold step: *He self-funded shows, rented theaters, and sold tickets directly to his niche audience.* That hustle proved he had a market—long before the industry took notice.

Now? Sold-out arenas. Netflix specials. Global tours.

Lesson: Own your niche, build your fan base, and the mainstream will chase you.

Math Break: How Many Fans Does It Take to Feed a Comic?

Spoiler: You don't need everybody to love you.

Let's say just 0.05% of the U.S. (around 17 million people) love your comedy and spend $35 a year on you.
That's $595 million in potential revenue.
If only 25% of them invest in you? That's still $140 million.

Let that sink in. Niche beats the mass-market every time.

Coaching Tip:
The Not-So-Fun Work That Pays Off

Finding your niche? That was fun. It was all about YOU.

Now it's time to do something truly radical.

Think about OTHER PEOPLE. (gasp!)

Yes, I know—you're already Googling "what do nerds like" while scrolling TikTok.

However, I promise that if you actually conduct this research, you'll be ahead of 90% of the comics who quit before payday.

Put in the effort. Reap the laughs. And eventually—the checks.

Coaching Tip:
RIP Tomato Steve

You've quit things before.
The herb garden that turned into weeds (except Steve, the tomato plant, who believed in you).

That one podcast where you interviewed your cat. (Solid guest, no follow-up episode.)

Don't let your comedy career be another half-finished hobby.
Stick with this. Do the research. Build the fan base.

Make people laugh so hard they want to throw money at you.
Now that's what I call harvesting comedy gold.

> ### What Agents Are Really Watching
>
> You think agents are watching you at that showcase?
>
> Nope. Agents are watching the audience. Why? Because if the room's dead, it doesn't matter how tight your set is. And they are specifically looking at who is laughing. If they are going to represent you, they need to know how to market you within a niche.
>
> Audience reaction builds careers.
>
> Agents know that. And now, so do you.

Exercise #9: Read the Room

In the chapters ahead, we will go beyond getting laughs and start building *genuine* connections with your audience. And connection begins with empathy. Empathy means shifting your mindset from "*I need you to laugh*" to "*I understand you.*"

Here's how to practice:

Step #1: Connect with strangers.

Go through the rest of today, paying attention to the small struggles people face—and name them out loud.

> **For instance:**
>
> *Yesterday at Home Depot, I noticed the cashier had no chair nearby. I said, "It must be hard standing on concrete all day. Why don't they give you a chair?" She lit up: "Yes! My back is killing me, and they don't care."*

> *When I handed my ticket to an underground parking attendant, I said, "It must be tough not seeing the sun all day." He beamed—because someone saw him.*

> *At an ice cream shop: "Does your right arm get sore from all that scooping?" Instant smile.*

So today, intentionally make a connection with three strangers by noticing a challenging aspect of their life and validating their experience. Tada! You just acquired your strongest superpower: empathy.

Step #2: Practice empathy onstage

Step one showed you how to connect by "seeing people." Now, let's use that same awareness on stage—to *read the room*.

One of the biggest mistakes comedians make is walking onstage and immediately making it all about *themselves*. The audience doesn't care (yet). They're still deciding if they like you, and that decision happens fast—within your first minute.

Your job in that first minute is to sense what they are feeling. What's going on with *them? What's happening in the room? What happened outside the club?*

Did everyone just circle for twenty minutes trying to find a parking spot?

Did the comic before you spill water on the front row?

Is everyone staring at the guy in the front row who has his feet up on the stage?

When you start by joking about what the *audience* is already thinking, you instantly connect—because you've joined their world instead of demanding they join yours.

For example, I once did a corporate gig where everyone had been partying hard the night before, and my show was at 8:30 a.m. I walked out and said:

"This is different. As a comic, I'm usually performing for people who are drunk—not people who are hungover."

Huge laugh. Why? Because I named the truth everyone in the room was already living.

That's what great comics do—they don't just *read the room*, they *speak the room's truth*.

Action Step:

Next time you perform, don't plan your opening. Leave room to read the room. If you want others to see *you*, see *them* first. Your comedy will hit deeper when your audience knows you don't just want their laughter—you care about their reality.

 **Next Up:** Find Your Audience Online

You've found your niche. In the next exercise, let's go one step further to find your audience. It's not just about recognizing the audience's laughter—it's about understanding where "your people" gather online, their passions and their problems, and how to authentically engage with them.

ELEMENT #2: YOUR AUDIENCE

—— Chapter 10 ——

Infiltrate Your Niche Audience Online

"If you can find comedy that is personal, it will resonate more with the audience."
—Robin Williams

Engage Your Audience—Without Acting Like You Need Therapy

Some call it stalking—I prefer to call it research. It's time to stop doom-scrolling and use your social media hours to identify, track, and attract your ideal people. Your Niche Audience is waiting!!!

>  **Coaching Tip:**
> **Don't Be That Date**
>
> The biggest turnoff for fans? Needy comics.
> They can smell it from the back row—the comic who's desperate for their approval, not a real connection.
>
> Comedy isn't a monologue.
> It's a conversation.
> It's about creating a shared, lived experience.
> If you're rattling off your set like a robot, you're not present. You're draining the room.
> If you're engaged, listening, reacting—you're building community and connection. That's star power.
>
> *Star power = connection power.*

Exercise #10:
Re-Introduce Yourself to Your Online Audience

Step #1: Out with the Old, In with the Niche

If your current social media is a mix of baby photos, vacation selfies, and your aunt's banana bread posts, it's time to start fresh. Create a new account (or repurpose an existing one) that's 100% focused on your *comedy niche*. This account should speak directly to your target audience—visually, verbally, and vibe-wise.

 **AI PROMPT: Here I Am!**
Let's use AI to help us again. Try this prompt:

Here's some info about me: [INSERT YOUR CREDENTIALS, COMEDY STYLE, LOCATION, and TARGET AUDIENCE]. [NICHE] is my new comedy niche. Please identify the social media platforms that are most active and popular among audiences interested in that niche.

Based on this information, please generate:

- 3–5 handle/usernames that reflect my niche and are likely available
- A short, funny, niche-relevant bio (under platform character limits)
- 5–10 niche-specific hashtags to help me reach the right audience
- A sample post that could introduce me and my niche to new followers
- Repeat for each relevant platform (Instagram, TikTok, YouTube, Facebook, LinkedIn, Twitter/X, etc.)

Coaching Tip:
No Buzz? Recheck the Niche

If you followed this step and your content is echoing in the void, your niche might be the problem. Some niches are gold mines with very active online communities (like teachers, mental health advocates, or sober moms), while others might be more like abandoned theme parks. You're riding that carousel on your own.

If you feel frustrated, go back to Exercise #7, where you used AI to review revenue possibilities for your niche and double-check that your niche has a real online presence. Use search tools: Type your niche into TikTok or Instagram and see if people are posting about it—and if those posts are getting views, comments, and shares. You're not just looking for any niche. You're looking for one that laughs back—and hires.

Step #2: Your First Post: A Funny Introduction

Your first post to engage with others in your niche should be a concise, engaging, and humorous introduction that captures your audience. Here are some easy formats:

- Video (Best Option): A short, engaging video where you introduce yourself in your comedic style. Keep it under 30–60 seconds.

Example:

"Hey, I'm [Your Name], and if you've ever [common problem(s) in your niche], then congratulations—you've survived! I'm here to make sure you laugh about it instead of crying. Follow me, or you'll be missing out on the best stress relief that doesn't involve tequila."

- Text Post with a Meme or Funny Image:
  - Post a meme or a funny image that relates to your niche.
  - Include a caption that sets the tone for your brand.
  - **Example:** If you're a funny plumber, post a meme of a DIY disaster and caption it:

    "If you think you can fix a leak with duct tape, you also probably think a 3-minute YouTube tutorial makes you a master plumber. Welcome to my world. Follow for more plumbing fails, laughs, and occasional life advice you never knew you needed."

> **Need a calendar for posting?**
> Go to the MMBF Workbook for a scheduling calendar for posting.

Step #3: Engage Your Early Adopters

The primary purpose of your account is to gain insight into your audience. Early followers are gold. Reach out and start a conversation. Ask them:
- What other comedians do you follow?
- What online groups do you belong to?
- Which platforms do you use the most?
- Respond to all legitimate comments.

> **Social Media Apps Can Help**
>
> You can also use SparkToro (with a free trial available), SocialBlade, or Iconosquare to discover what your target audience reads, watches, and follows. Then focus your comedy on topics that are already part of the conversation.

Step #4: Facebook & Reddit Recon

- Join five Facebook groups related to your niche and actively engage with them. Think of yourself as a comedy spy (but with more emojis).
- Dive into subreddits relevant to your niche. Observe which topics get the most upvotes—this can be comedy gold.

Step #5: Keep Track of What You Learn

Write down:

- **Demographics**: Who are they? Age, gender, location?
- **Preferred Social Media**: Where do they hang out?
- **Language: Gen Z slang?** Industry jargon? Swear words?
- **What They Love:** What posts get the most love?
- **Organizations:** What groups do they belong to? (Some might hire you!)
- **Complaints & Pain Points:** What pisses them off? Comedy thrives on shared frustrations.

> **Coaching Tip:**
> **Turn-offs That Make Them Tune Out**
>
> - **LOOK AT ME, I'M FUNNY!** Hold back on jokes at first—one insensitive comment can get you ghosted.
> - **LOOK AT ME, I'M SELLING THINGS!** Engage before self-promoting—nobody likes a spammer. No lecturing.

By getting to know your audience and engaging regularly, you're on course to build a loyal fan base. Later in this book, I will focus on creating content for them, but for now, I just want you to establish your account, do preliminary research on your followers, and read the comments of others who post in your niche. We're just getting started, laying the groundwork for engagement and your comedy "customers!"

Now, get out there and channel your inner comedy spy!

 **Next Up:** Let's meet the comic already paving the way for your success.

ELEMENT #2: YOUR AUDIENCE

— Chapter 11 —

Blueprint Your Breakout—
How to Hijack Your Rival's Audience

• • • • • • • • • • • •

"Don't waste your energy on being jealous.
Be better. Be funnier.
Create something that makes people jealous of you."

—TINA FEY

• • • • • • • • • • • •

The Jealousy Trap: A Reality Check

Jealousy won't get you gigs, but a strategic approach will.

If you're smart, you'll stop looking at your successful competitors with envy and start using them as blueprints, not barriers. You can learn from their mistakes, leverage their momentum, and *transform their audience into your audience*. Let's ride some coattails—*strategically*.

Let's be honest—comedians have a love-hate relationship with other comics who "make it." Have you ever seen someone doing material similar to yours and blowing up while you're still hustling for a drink ticket? Yeah. It's not cute.

I'll admit it: I once stewed over a fellow female comic who skyrocketed to fame. When she changed her number, I took it as a personal affront.

Our friendship faded faster than my dream of winning an Oscar for Best Original Screenplay and Best Actress in the same year.

Then years later, we were booked on the same show—and guess what? She thought *I* had ghosted *her*. Turns out, even after you've made it, you still need real friends who won't roll their eyes when you're overwhelmed by "Which beachfront property should I buy?"

To quote the poet The Notorious B.I.G., "Mo money, mo problems."

Jealousy is a dead-end. Strategy is a superpower. So don't stew—study. Don't copy—*reverse-engineer*. And don't hate—*hijack another comic's blueprint and build your own path.*

"The first rule of success: Don't hate on other people's success. If someone is doing better than you, shut up, take notes, and figure out how they did it."

—Joan Rivers

Case Study: Riding Coattails Like a Pro

Dan Nainan was a former tech guy who took my comedy workshop. I saw his potential and advised him to lean into the Indian-American tech niche—mainly because he was based in Silicon Valley, surrounded by his ideal audience.

At the time, **Russell Peters** was the breakout Indian comic. Dan didn't compete—he studied. He created clean, cultural material with a twist: his own Japanese-Indian background.

One night, Russell Peters was headlining a club. When the manager needed a quick fill-in act, Dan pounced:

"Put me on—I'm Indian too. I can work this crowd."

He crushed it. Russell's team noticed. Soon, Dan was opening for him, and his comedy career exploded.

> **Lesson:** Instead of sitting in the back row
> hating someone else's success,
> position yourself to be part of it.
> Use their momentum to jump-start your own.

Learn From—Don't Copy—Your Competition

Is someone in your niche already doing well? Great. That means your niche is *viable.*

Your job: Do it differently. Do it better. Do it like only you can.

You may be a funny teacher, lawyer, parent, engineer, or guy who lives in a tiny house and makes sourdough. Whatever it is, your flavor is unique. Your competitors aren't roadblocks; they're *proof of concept.*

Coaching Tip:

Borrow Their Hustle, Not Their Punchlines.

Using another comedian for inspiration is smart.

Stealing their material? That's breaking the one sacred rule of comedy:

Thou shalt not steal.

Exercise #11:
Find Your Blueprint to Success

Step #1: Identify Comedians In Your Niche

In **Exercise #7**: Rate and Rank Them All, *you already used AI to define your comedy niche. Now, let's go deeper.*

Ask AI This:

"Give me a list of 5 mid-level comedians who brand themselves as [INSERT YOUR NICHE] comics—such as teacher comedy, lawyer comedy, ADHD comedy, etc. Only include comedians who are making money from comedy, including: live shows, content, brand partnerships, social media income, or writing gigs."

Select the ones that feel most aligned with your vibe.

Step #2: Analyze Their Blueprint

Grab your Accountability Buddy and share the comics you each found. Watch their live performances and check out their social media, then ask your Buddy:

- How does my social media differ from the comic?
- What part of their act resonates with you, and you think relates to me, too?
- How am I different from them?
- How am I the same?
- What makes me different from them?

Coaching Tip:
Hobby or Career?

If you search your niche and nobody is making money in it, you haven't struck comedy gold—you've found a hobby. Cute for open mics, terrible for your bank account. Pick a niche that can make you stand out and earn you money.

Step #3: Stalk Strategically

Follow them. Like their posts. Leave comments.
Not in a stalker way. In a strategic way.
Notice:

- What posts get the most engagement?
- What gets shared and what gets ignored?
- What jokes or themes light up their comments section?
- Which content gets applause, praise, and shares?

Apply the patterns. Then remix them through your own lens.

Step #4: Set Google Alerts on Your Niche

As you did in a previous exercise, set Google Alerts for:

- Your niche
- Your Blueprint comedian(s)
- Events or gigs they're landing.

Stay in the loop and ride those trend waves as they come.

Step #5: Reverse Engineer Your Blueprint

Out of the list you made above, choose the one comedian who most embodies the kind of success you want and use them as your Blueprint for Success. You're not copying their jokes; you're studying their moves. Like a coach analyzing game tape. What did they get right? What did they do wrong? How can you improve on what they created?

AI PROMPT: Use [COMEDIAN'S NAME] As The Blueprint For My Career

"Analyze the career of [INSERT COMEDIAN'S NAME] and create a step-by-step blueprint I can adapt as a [YOUR NICHE] comedian.

Break it down by:

- How did they start?
- Major career moves and pivots
- Revenue streams (stand-up, merch, podcasts, TV, etc.)
- Pivotal gigs or breakthroughs
- Challenges they faced and how they overcame them
- What platforms or strategies did they use to grow their audience?

**Coaching Tip:
You're Not a Knockoff.**

This isn't about becoming a knockoff version of someone else. It's about understanding the business moves behind the funny—and adapting those strategies to fit your voice, your audience, and your path. It's like how bicyclists draft off each other to help each other win.

Here's where I'm at:

- I've been doing comedy for [X] years
- I have [X] followers
- My biggest highlight so far is [YOUR MOMENT]
- My comedy niche is [YOUR NICHE]

Step #6: Your First Leads List

Looking over your new **Blueprint for Success**, take note of:

- The venues where your Blueprint Comic has performed.
- Who hired them—companies, colleges, conferences?
- Which producers, directors, writers, collaborators work with them on the regular?

This is your leads list. You'll use this to pitch yourself later.

>  **Coaching Tip:**
> **Stealing Clients (Not Material)**
>
> Check your Blueprint's website. Find client testimonials. These are paying customers who already love your niche. Reach out and pitch yourself for next year's event.

Step #7: Hijack their followers—Here's How

Gentle Infiltration:

- Start showing up in their comment section—not as a troll, but as the funnier friend creating connections.

  Examples:

  "This killed me. As someone who's also dated someone similar—I created a support group—it's called my act."

  "Relatable! I just posted a video about surviving this exact disaster."

- Post 5–7 clever comments over one week.
- Reply kindly when fans engage with you.
- Invite them to your own post, clip, or free mini-event.

Strategic Commenting:

Pick high-engagement posts and post a memorable, helpful reply (not a plug).

- Template: Short joke → tiny resource → signature

  Example: "If your boss ghosted you, tell them 'I wrote you a missing-person report: found—still angry.'"

Why it works: fans notice the funny helper and will click your profile.

Event pitch (bio or post):

"Free Live: 'If you liked [rival]'s bit about [insert], you'll love my set about that as well, but with a therapy degree and worse decisions. Friday 7 pm—bring wine. Link in bio.'"

Be the Useful Comic:

Fans follow comedians for the laughs and the sense of community. Give them both:

- Free micro-value: "3 one-liners about [Blueprint Comic's big theme]" PDF.
- Post it where rival fans hang and pin it in your bio for easy access. Script for post: "If you think [Blueprint Comic's theme] is wild, here are three jokes you can say to your ex at brunch. Free, no judgment—drop a 🖤 to get it."

Step #8: Take an action

Now that you've done the research, write it out:

- What topics will *you* focus on?
- Which *gigs* excite you most?
- What *niche content* will speak to *your* people? And aligns with your WHY?
- How are you connecting with your Blueprint's followers?

This isn't just a dream board. *It's your business plan.*

Now take action. This action can be a social media post or a new bit of material.

> **Coaching Tip:**
> At this point in the book, if you're having a hard time taking action, you might want to do the "Mindset" exercises at the end of this book.

Final Note: Blueprint, Don't Xerox

The goal isn't to *become* your Blueprint—it's to learn from them. Their success can fast-track yours—*if* you stay true to yourself.

 **Next Up**: Let's take your vision and test it where your fans live: *Online*.

ELEMENT #3: YOUR PLATFORM

—— Chapter 12 ——

Post. Bomb. Repeat:
The Social Media Strategy for Comics Who Want to Get Paid

"If you want to be a comedian, start putting stuff out there. You don't need permission. You need Wi-Fi."
—A𝐧drew Schulz

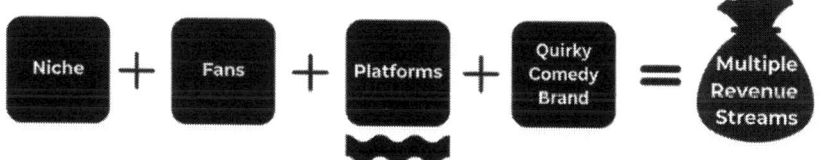

Why Social Media Is the New Comedy Club

You've nailed your niche, you know your audience, and you've scoped out the competition. Now it's time to get famous within your niche. How? By treating social media like your personal comedy club.

Back in the day, comedy clubs held the keys to success. Now? Clubs prioritize comedians with strong online platforms. Got followers? You get booked. Don't? Enjoy performing for drink tickets and "exposure."

Even if you're headlining, gigs alone won't pay your rent. Clubs refine material, but they won't make you rich. That's where social media steps in. A built-in audience means bookers, agents, and managers notice you. Being a comedian without a social media presence is like telling your best joke into a canyon—lots of echoes, no audience.

> **Bring Your Own Audience (Seriously)**
>
> "Headlining a comedy club, I was surprised when the club owner asked me what I was going to do to get an audience. That's when I realized that bringer shows don't stop when you're the headliner. These days, clubs don't care if you're funny; they care if you're followable. If you can't fill seats, you'd better at least fill a TikTok trend."
>
> —**Ophira Eisenberg**

The Synergy Between Live Shows and Social Media

Some comics believe that going viral means they can abandon live performances. Wrong. Social media and live shows fuel each other. Followers buy tickets, and live audiences boost your online presence.

"I didn't wait for someone to cast me. I cast myself—on YouTube."
—Bo Burnham

Viral fame gets people in the door. A killer live show keeps them coming back.

>  **Coaching Tip:**
> **The Social Media vs. Stand-Up Divide**
>
> Many touring comics complain about social media influencers taking stage time. But here's the truth: *being funny for 60 seconds online is not the same as commanding a live audience for an hour.*
>
> While some influencers bomb on stage, they still *fill seats*, and in today's comedy business, that matters. If you want a sustainable career, you need more than viral clips—you need a *strong, personal act* that translates to a live audience.
>
> Instead of seeing influencers as competition, take notes. They master engagement, branding, and audience building. Combine their social strategies with your stand-up chops, and you've got the *ultimate comedy power* move.

Success Story: Trevor Wallace—Viral Sensation to Comedy Mogul

At 27, Trevor Wallace turned *short-form viral videos* into a multi-million-dollar comedy empire. His niche, which includes parodies of Gen-Z stereotypes, has racked up *20 million followers*. One ten-second clip—just him walking into a car drunk—hit *42 million views*.

His earnings? *$74.9K/month from YouTube alone*, plus brand sponsorships, merch, and *sold-out comedy club tours*. That's how you *convert likes into laughs—and cash*.

Your Platforms: A Comedian's Guide to Owning the Digital Stage

The days of waiting for a late-night show spot to "make it" are over. Today, comedians get famous by mastering digital platforms. Currently, here are the platforms popular as of the writing of this book:

YouTube: The Gateway to Big Opportunities

- Where Issa Rae launched *Awkward Black Girl*, leading to HBO's *Insecure*.
- Offers in-depth analytics on your audience.
- **Example:** Rachel Ballinger built 2.75M subscribers from *You Know What Pisses Me Off?* and transitioned into stand-up.

Instagram: Visual Comedy Gold

- Stories and Reels let you test jokes fast.
- Gabriel Iglesias dominates Instagram with humor as big as his Volkswagen bus collection.

TikTok: The Viral Playground

- Where trends are born for all entertainers.
- Lil Nas X rode TikTok analytics to make the "Old Town Road" song a hit.

Websites & Email: The Old-School Essentials

- A website is your professional calling card.
- Email lists provide direct access to your fans.

> "The internet has made it so much easier to find your specific audience. Nobody is truly for everyone, and now you don't have to be."
>
> —Taylor Tomlinson

Comedians Who Mastered the Game

Jessica Kirson: Niche + Social Media = Sold-Out Tours

Her crowd work clips exploded online. At 55, she leaned into her *NYC/Jewish/Lesbian/Mom* niche, leading to her **Never-Ending Tour** and Netflix specials.

Andrew Schulz: Comedy's Digital Mogul

Schulz went *all-in* on YouTube after getting ignored by TV networks. His *self-produced specials, podcasts, and edgy humor now rake in $10M+ a year.*

Nurse John: TikTok Star to Comedy Tour Headliner

A Filipino nurse in Canada started making *funny healthcare videos* during the pandemic. Now, he's on a *sold-out North American comedy tour.*

So, what's a comedian to do? Simple: think beyond the club. Think beyond agents. DIY your career.

Exercise #12: Build Your Social Media Strategy (Without Losing Your Mind)

Not sure where to start? Let AI take the wheel—no overpriced social media manager required.

Step #1: Choose Your Path

- **The Expensive Way:** Hire a social media manager ($$$, they won't get your voice and might ghost you mid-launch).
- **The Smart Way:** Use successful comedians in your niche as a blueprint—but post your original content.
- **The Easiest Way:** Use AI to build a custom strategy in seconds.

Step #2: Check in With You

Before diving in, ask yourself:

- Which platforms look fun?
- What does content feel like to you?
- What are you excited (or at least willing) to try first?

Trust your gut—it's got better taste than the algorithm.

Step #3: AI Prompt: Research & Refine Your Social Media Strategy

Ask AI This

Prompt #1: *Deep Dive on My Blueprint Comic's Social Media Strategy*

I've identified [name of blueprint comedian] as a model for my niche, which is INSERT YOUR NICHE. Help me analyze their current social media presence. What platforms do they use? What types of posts get the most engagement? What formats (stand-up clips, sketches, rants, clips from live performances, etc.) work best for them? Provide a platform-by-platform breakdown, along with suggested post lengths for each platform.

Step #4: Your Turn Now

Prompt #2: *Getting Started Ask AI This:*

I'm a [age], [gender], [niche] comedian just getting started with social media for my niche. Personally, the social media platforms that I use daily are [INSERT YOUR FAVORITE PLATFORMS]. My favorite things to post are [insert what you enjoy posting, e.g., direct-to-camera content, clips of live performances, sketches, tips, and advice, etc.]. Please recommend one to two platforms that align with my niche and style. Also, based on [competitor comedian] as inspiration, suggest a few simple content ideas I can post this month, a low-stress way to engage with potential followers in my niche, and a couple of first steps I can take this week—without burning out.

(That prompt just saved you $5,000. You're welcome.)

Step #5: Post Already!

Strategy means nothing without action. Start now—no fancy gear. No overthinking.

Use what AI suggested:

- **If it said YouTube:** Post clips and commentaries.
- **If it said TikTok:** Quick sketches or crowd work moments.
- **If it said Twitch:** Go live, be weird, engage.

Just post something for 5 days in a row.
See what hits. Double down on what gets likes or laughs

Now get out there. Your fans are scrolling. Let's build your comedy empire, one post at a time.

**Coaching Tip:
Just Post!**

Everyone has fantastic ideas, but ideas without action just don't exist. Some apps can help you actually *post* instead of just *plan*. For instance, Castmagic.io automatically turns your videos or podcasts into ready-to-post clips, captions, and social content—like having a virtual assistant who never complains about your punchlines.

Scared? Social media is kinder than bombing on stage. If a post flops? Delete it. If someone trolls you? Block and move on. Nobody remembers a bad post.

You won't go viral overnight. But TAG me, and I'll see your post—*unless you procrastinate and I'm dead.* Just hashtag #MMBF.

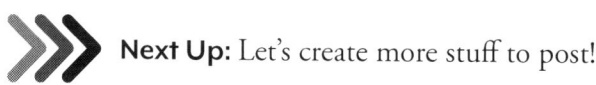

Next Up: Let's create more stuff to post!

ELEMENT #3: YOUR PLATFORM

—— Chapter 13 ——

Platform Tailored Content

• • • • • • • • • • • •

"The bottom line is: I take social media seriously, and I'm not ducking around."

—CHELSEA HANDLER

• • • • • • • • • • • •

Why "Come See My Show" is Useless (and What to Do Instead)

Let's be clear: Social media is not your digital billboard—it's a cocktail party, and you're trying to be the funniest guest. The *worst* post you can make?

"Hey, come see my show!"

No one cares.

Instead of begging for attention, give your niche audience what they came for: jokes, relatable struggles, mini-meltdowns, and oddly specific rants that make their day better—or at least distract them from their 87 unread work emails.

Golden Rule of Social Media: It's not about you. It's about *them*.

Make your content platform-specific and audience-focused. The more you understand each platform's vibe, the more likely your posts are to actually connect.

>  **Coaching Tip:**
> **Social Media Pitfalls**
>
> Social media can launch your career, and it's a great place to experiment, but it can also get you canceled faster than a joke that starts with, "White people have it hard!" Be thoughtful in your posts.
>
> - **Michael Richards (a.k.a. Kramer)** tanked his career with a racist rant in 2006.
> - **Jenna Marbles**, a YouTube pioneer, walked away in 2020 after problematic past content resurfaced.
>
> *Lesson:*
> Go for *longevity*, not cheap shock value.
> Think of your content like your comedy—funny now, but also worth watching later (without needing an apology video).

Understanding Content Formats

Now, let's figure out how to post your brilliance in the *correct format* for the *right platform*—because doing stand-up on LinkedIn is a red flag (unless your niche is "HR nightmares").

What You Post and Where You Post It:

Format	Best Platforms
Stand-Up Clips	TikTok, Instagram Reels, YouTube Shorts
Satirical News	YouTube, TikTok
Interactive Comedy	Instagram Live, Threads

Behind-the-Scenes	Instagram Stories, Facebook
Sketch Comedy	TikTok, YouTube Shorts
Parodies	TikTok, YouTube
To-Camera Opinion Pieces	TikTok, Instagram, Facebook Stories
Funny Interviews	TikTok, Instagram, YouTube

Coaching Tip:

Don't overthink. Just post. The algorithm rewards consistent effort, not perfection. The more you post, the faster you learn what hits.

Match Your Niche to the Right Platform

What you like watching might not be what your audience needs from you. Match your niche to where your audience already scrolls:

- **Corporate Humor & Keynotes:** YouTube playlists, TikTok bite-sized tips, Instagram Reels
- **Comedy Writers & Workshop Hosts:** TikTok, Instagram Lives, Email blasts
- **Sports Fanatics:** Facebook Groups, YouTube deep dives
- **Authors & Tip-Givers:** TikTok & Instagram with funny mini-lessons
- **Older Audiences:** Personal stories on Facebook; niche groups

Exercise #13: Write Material Specific to Your Niche & Platform

Ask AI This:

"List the top 10 problems or frustrations that [INSERT NICHE] are currently dealing with. Include details that these people would find hard, weird, scary, or stupid." Example: If my niche is teachers, they might be frustrated with *"lack of funding." "Not getting tenure." "Dated textbooks."*

Once you have a list of your niche's pain points, get together with your Accountability Buddy and see if you can find something funny about these problems to post on social media as a meme, a sketch, or a commentary.

Now decide:

- What format will it take? (Clip, sketch, meme, rant, news parody, etc.)
- Which platform is best suited for that content?

AI Hack: Let Tech Do the Brainstorming

Prompt:

I'm a [age] [gender] comedian creating content for the [niche]. My audience cares about [insert many of your niche audience's pain points you've discovered and have written material about]. Help me brainstorm a month of content (posting every other day) for [platform], utilizing stand-up clips, sketches, personal stories, and trending topics relevant to my niche, as well as telling me the best platforms to use.

Example:

Plumbing Comedy

- TikTok: "The 3 Funniest Calls Plumbers Get" (30-sec reenactments)
- YouTube: Longform commentary with bloopers
- Instagram: Behind-the-scenes before gigs at plumbing trade shows

> **Plan Like a Pro**
>
> Use the *MMBF Workbook* to create a content calendar to map out your posts ahead of time. Don't wing it like that guy who forgot he was headlining until showtime.

Repurpose Like a Pro: Post Once, Share Everywhere

Don't burn out trying to create unique content for every platform. Repurpose it instead.

Record a sketch or rant on TikTok, then use **SnapTik** (or a similar free app) to remove the watermark so you can repost it on Instagram Reels, YouTube Shorts, and Facebook without looking like you only exist on TikTok.

Pro Tips for Repurposing:

- **Same video, new caption:** Reframe the text for the platform's vibe.
- **Adjust the intro:** Hook YouTube viewers with a longer setup, while TikTok needs an instant punch.
- **Captions & Hashtags:** Adapt them for platform-specific trends and searchability.
- **Post Timing:** Spread content out instead of dropping it everywhere at once.

You don't need to reinvent yourself. Just **refresh the packaging**.

> **Tools for Comedy Content Success**
>
> - **Write Niche Jokes**—Content that hits the people in your niche where they live (mentally).
> - **Collaborate**—Find others in your niche and cross-promote with them.
> - **Use Polls**—Crowdsource jokes and topics from your audience.
> - **Jump on Trends**—But give it your spin.
> - **Repurpose Smartly**—One joke = tweet + sketch + rant.
> - **Cross-Promote**—Tease YouTube clips on TikTok, or vice versa.
> - **AI Tools**—Utilize ChatGPT to generate ideas for titles, hashtags, and captions.
> - **SnapTik & Friends**—Remove watermarks and keep your content brand-neutral.

FINAL THOUGHT: It's a Two-Way Street

You'll start out throwing spaghetti at the algorithm—and that's okay. However, keep refining based on *what your audience responds to*, not just what feels enjoyable to you.

The goal? Make your people laugh *online* so they'll show up *offline*—with tickets in hand and friends in tow.

Now go post. Seriously. Your fans are out there—scrolling, lurking, and waiting to hit the like button.

 **Next Up:** Fall in Love with Your Followers

ELEMENT #3: YOUR PLATFORM

— Chapter 14 —

Work the Crowd, Win the Fans

• • • • • • • • • • • •

"Crowd work is like social media in real life. If you listen, react, and roll with the unexpected, you build a connection. If you just stand there waiting for laughs, you're a telemarketer with a mic."

—Big Jay Oakerson

• • • • • • • • • • • •

Your Followers Are More Than Just Numbers

If you're staring at your follower count like it's a casino slot machine, waiting for it to hit the jackpot, you're missing the point. Those aren't just numbers—they're people. And if you're not engaging them, your social media is as dead as a Tuesday night open mic at a bar with three drunk guys and a broken microphone.

Social media isn't just content—it's a *relationship*. And like any good relationship, the love must flow both ways. You want them to click "love"? You've got to *engage with them* first. Reply to their comments, react to their posts, and acknowledge their insights.

Because if you're just standing on the digital stage shouting into the void, you're one bad post away from being ghosted.

Digital Crowd Work: Turning Followers Into Fans

Let's talk about crowd work for a second. Gone are the days when stand-up was a one-way street—comics tossing jokes into the void and hoping for laughs. These days, audiences want *interaction*.

Think about pros like **Big Jay Oakerson, Judy Gold**, and **Maz Jobrani**. They don't just open their sets with a generic "How's everybody doing?" They *engage*, riff, and react in real time. It's personal, spontaneous, and comedy gold.

Now, take that same energy and apply it to *social media*. The digital stage isn't just a place to *dump content*—it's where you *start* conversations.

- Instead of just posting a clip of your set, *ask a question*.
- Instead of dropping a joke and logging off, *stick around and reply to comments*.
- Instead of treating social media like a billboard, *treat it like an open mic with an interactive audience*.

> Your audience wants to be involved. Give them **a reason to engage.**

The Sweet Spot: Social Media Success Benchmarks

Want to be taken seriously? Industry insiders look for these numbers:

- **Instagram**—50K+ for small venues, 200K+ for major clubs.
- **YouTube**—100K subscribers get noticed; 500K+ means serious offers.
- **TikTok**—100K–200K followers opens doors; 500K+ secures the big leagues.
- **Total Online Following**—A combined 200K+ across platforms? Agents and bookers start calling.

Currently, TikTok pays creators with over 10,000 followers based on the number of hits their videos receive, which must be one minute or longer.

But it's not just about numbers—it's about engagement. Followers don't matter if they're not buying tickets.

"Crowd work isn't just talking to the audience—it's making them feel like they're part of the show. That's when the real magic happens."

—JESSICA KIRSON

Coaching Sidebar: Get Spontaneous and Go Live!

I'm not a natural poster—I didn't grow up with social media. However, when I begrudgingly started *Instagram Live comedy workshops*, I was blown away by the response and its impact on book sales and workshop registrations.

It also expanded my reach globally. I met Syrian comics, first-time comedians, and people with *wild* stories. As a result, my book sales *skyrocketed*, and I secured *book deals in seven countries, private gigs, and a growing fan base*. No joke!

Try going live and see what happens.

Exercise #14:
Ignite Your Engagement Game

Here are some powerful ways to engage followers on and off social media and build a fanbase that buys tickets, not just follows you.

Pick at least three to do this week:

On Social Media:

Interactive Polls and Questions (*Instagram Stories, X/Twitter*)

Ask fans to vote on punchlines, guess the ending of a joke, or share niche-specific experiences. For example:

- **Women's Issues:** "Best unwritten rule of a girls' night out? A) 'We leave together' B) 'No judgment on tequila decisions' C) 'Emergency makeup kit required.'"

- **Boomer Humor:** "What's the most boomer way to answer the phone? A) 'Yello?' B) 'This is Bob speaking' C) 'Hello, who's calling?' D) 'Hold on, let me get my glasses.'"

- **Accounting Comedy**: "Biggest tax season horror story? Drop your best one below!"

- **Healthcare Humor:** "Nurses, what's the weirdest thing a patient has ever asked you?"

- **Christian Comedy:** "Most awkward moment in church?
    A) Singing the wrong verse alone.
    B) Accidentally saying 'You too' when the pastor blesses you.
    C) Dozing off during the sermon and waking up to 'Amen.'"

- **Live Q&A Sessions** (YouTube, Instagram Live, TikTok Live)

- **Host themed Q&As**—"Sales Nightmares and Cold Call Fails" or "Ask a Nurse Anything—But Please, No WebMD."

- **Fan-Inspired Content** (TikTok, YouTube, Instagram Reels)
  Reenact followers' funniest work mishaps: the most cringe-worthy HR meeting, the ridiculous patient complaint, the worst first date after divorce, or the most absurd thing a well-meaning church lady has said to you.

- **Behind-the-Scenes Content** (Instagram, YouTube, TikTok)
  Show bloopers, writing sessions, or backstage moments at a show—people love the process.

- **Funny Response Videos** (TikTok Duets, Instagram Reels)
  React to audience-submitted stories and comments. Social media makes this easy to do with one click. If someone shares a *bad customer service* horror story, act it out in the most dramatic way possible.

- **Crowdsourced Jokes or Sketches** (Twitter, Instagram)
  Let followers give you *three random words* related to their industry and challenge yourself to write a joke on the spot.

Off Social Media:

- **Exclusive Fan Meetups** (Patreon, Live Shows)
  Host pre-show or post-show meetups for superfans who follow your niche.

- **Comedy Workshops or Webinars** (Zoom, Patreon)
  Offer "Sell Like a Comedian" workshops for sales teams or "Tax Deductions So Funny They Should Be Illegal" sessions for accountants.

- **Personalized Video Messages** (Cameo, Patreon)
  Send funny, customized shoutouts to fans—like a *"boomer dad" video for Gen X followers* explaining how to reset a router.

- **Interactive Comedy Shows**
  Pull *audience topics live* or stream shows for online fans to interact.

- **Custom Merchandise with Fan Input**
  Let fans vote on funny niche-specific merch slogans.

- **Community Initiatives or Charity Tie-Ins**
  Run campaigns where a percentage of show profits supports healthcare worker wellness programs, women's shelters, or financial literacy initiatives.

At the end of the week, meet with your Buddy and ask each other:

- Which content got the most engagement?
- How did followers react to direct interaction?
- What was surprising about their responses?

> The more you post, the more engagement you'll have, and the more followers you'll gain. Daily post every day. Hell—post 3 times a day. Don't kill your momentum by being a perfectionist. Just keep posting.

**Coaching Tip:
Don't Keep It to Yourself**

Share your results with your audience! For example, if you ran a poll about toilet paper dads, post: "Turns out only 12% of dads are brave enough to replace the toilet paper roll. Comedy gold, am I right?"

FINAL THOUGHT: Engage, Adapt, Repeat

Your audience isn't just *watching*—they're part of the show. The more you engage, the more they invest in *you*.

Don't just post—*connect*. Build relationships, make them laugh, and turn them from *followers into superfans*.

 **Next Up:** Let's get Analytical

ELEMENT #3: YOUR PLATFORM

— Chapter 15 —

Crush It with Analytics

• • • • • • • • • • • • •

"Analytics is a tool that helped me grow, and it helps you reach your audience. I'll never stop using it."

—**Connor Wood,**
TRANSITIONED FROM VIRAL CONTENT TO
A SUCCESSFUL STAND-UP COMEDY CAREER

• • • • • • • • • • • • •

Why Metrics Are Your Secret Weapon

By now, if you've been following along and doing the exercises in this book, you've hopefully been posting about your niche and engaging with your audience like a pro. But if your follower count still looks like the sperm count of an eighty-five-year-old man, don't panic—it's time to dive into your social media analytics and figure out what's hitting and what's tanking.

Analytics and feedback are the closest thing to that instant audience reaction you get on stage. When you're performing live, you know immediately if a joke lands or bombs. Online? That same feedback loop exists—it's called analytics, and trust me, it's your best friend. And it's not as scary as getting on a scale.

Obsessing over your metrics is like wielding the Eye of Sauron for your comedy career—all-knowing and a little terrifying, but worth it. You know exactly what's working and what's flopping. More importantly, how to tweak your act to reach the people who care. Asking another comic, "Hey, what do you think?" is all well and good, but analytics don't lie—they give you cold, hard facts. And in a business where your next gig depends on not only getting laughs, but filling seats, you need every edge you can get.

> If your follower count looks like the sperm count of an eighty-five-year-old man, don't panic—it's time to dive into your social media analytics and figure out what's hitting and what's tanking.

Apps, Tools, and Help
(Because You're Not a Data Scientist)

Numerous analytical and feedback tools are available to facilitate this process. Visit **judycarter.com** for a comprehensive list of tools and apps. And if this all sounds like a trip to Nerdville and you'd rather focus on writing jokes, don't sweat it. You can hire people to do the data deep dive for you. Numbers may not be funny, but getting paid definitely is.

Your Data's Talking—Are You Listening?

Think of analytics as digital heckling, but instead of shouting, "You suck!" it's saying, "Hey, maybe don't post that gerbil joke again, nobody's laughing." It shows you who's watching your stuff, where they live, their age, gender, and even what time of day they're most likely to double-tap your post. It's like having a superpower to see into the minds of your audience.

Real-Life Example: It's Never Too Late to Score Big

Leanne Morgan didn't blow up in comedy clubs—she built her empire from living rooms. Starting by performing at jewelry parties in rural Tennessee, she used the captive female audience as a testing ground for her humor, joking about motherhood, breastfeeding, and everyday life. That down-home, women-only humor became her niche. Years later, when she was a grandmother in her 50s, she leaned into posting those kinds of stories online—and one clip about concerts with "old people" and aching feet went viral, racking up over 30 million views in a week. Overnight, she had built a national fan base. By studying her analytics—specifically, where her followers lived—she was able to route tours directly to the cities where her fans were waiting. Add in a social media team and a steady stream of content, and Morgan went from jewelry parties to selling out theaters across the country, building millions of online followers, and ultimately landing her own Netflix sitcom with Chuck Lorre. Proof that knowing your niche, testing your material, and letting analytics guide your next move can turn everyday jokes into a multimillion-dollar career.

Data or Die: The Comedian's Guide to Going Viral

> ### Riding Trend Waves to Go Viral
>
> Visit Google Trends to see what people are searching for. Relate it to your niche. If you're an LGBTQ comic and a TV show is trending, mash that up with a post about a gay character in the show—you just might go viral.
>
> - **Be Consistent with Posting:** Stay in your audience's feed by posting frequently.
>
> - **Create a Hook in the First Few Seconds:** Start with something attention-grabbing—no fluff.
>
> - **Be Authentic and Vulnerable:** Audiences love real, relatable comedians. Self-deprecating humor and personal stories build connections.
>
> - **Engage with Your Audience:** Respond to comments, solicit feedback, and transform interactions into valuable content.
>
> - **Utilize Music and Sound Effects** to enhance comedic timing and boost discoverability.
>
> - **Use Captions or Subtitles:** Essential for accessibility and engagement.
>
> - **Tap Into Emotional or Thought-Provoking Humor:** Content that resonates with the heart or sparks thought can go viral.

> **Laughter & Tears**
>
> Vulnerability and authenticity draw people in—the laughter and the tears bring them back for more. For example, here is a post from a teacher:
>
> *"Today, during recess, one of my students sat next to me on the bench, swinging his legs and staring at his shoes. I asked what was up. He shrugged and said, 'Nothing.' Classic kid response. But then he looked up and whispered, 'Miss, my mom didn't have enough money for lunch today, so I gave her my lunch money instead. I'll just eat when I get home.'*
>
> *Cue me, holding back tears, immediately offering him my granola bar like it was the last piece of bread on the Titanic. He smiled and took it, then casually said, 'But don't worry, Miss, I don't even like school lunch anyway.'"*
>
> Teaching is full of these moments—hilarious, heartbreaking, and humbling all at once. If anyone's looking for a reason why teachers fight for free lunch programs, it's because kids shouldn't have to choose between eating and helping their parents. Also, I need to start carrying more snacks.
>
> #TeachingLife #FeedTheKids #HumorWithHeart

- **Promote User-Generated Content:** Encourage followers to remix or react to your content, creating a viral loop.
- **Use Hashtags Wisely:** Make them relevant to your content, not just generic #comedy hashtags.

Exercise #15:
Metrics, Mayhem, and Making It Big

Now let's get down to the dirty work. Time to figure out who's watching your stuff and how you can tweak your content to blow up your follower count.

> **Deep Dive in the Workbook**
>
> Social media platforms already have great analytics tools, but some third-party apps and platforms can serve as your digital partner. They are listed in the workbook along with a calendar posting guide for your social media.

Step #1: Run Analytics on Your Audience

In Element #2 Exercise #11: Find Your Blueprint to Success, you've gotten to know your audience by digging into your Blueprint Comic's followers, reading comments, going on Reddit, and engaging with them in Facebook Groups. Now, let's look at your followers. Use the social media analytics tool that comes with your app. Write down the following:

- **Age range** of your audience:
- **Gender** breakdown:
- **Location** (cities/countries):
- **Time** they are most active:

Step #2: Work Hard & Work Smart

Although I've suggested it repeatedly, it's worth giving engagement with your audience another try. Now that you know who your people are, think about how to tweak your content to lock them in:

- What time will you post now that you know when they're online?

- What content will you double down on based on the highest engagement posts?
- What will you stop posting? (Not everything works—cut the duds.)

Step #3: Refine Your Niche

Based on your metrics, how will you further refine your niche? What adjustments will you make in your content? (Maybe you're a funny plumber, but you're realizing your "parenting while fixing pipes" content gets more traction—lean into it!)

Step #4: Use AI to Rewrite Your Online Bio

Just know that you will *always* be discovering new ways to promote yourself online, and that means rewriting your online bio to keep up with the changes you've made, as you view your metrics and grow into your niche. So, it's time to redo the bio you wrote in Exercise #10: Reintroduce Yourself to Your Online Audience. Use the same prompt but add new elements you've discovered.

Coaching Tip:
Experiment with Something New

Take those numbers and experiment like a mad scientist—maybe a plumbing-themed TikTok dance or a live Q&A about your grossest gig. Test it, analyze it, and see how your audience reacts.

FINAL THOUGHT: Data Drives Dollars

Analytics isn't just for the nerds—it's for anyone serious about making comedy a career. The more you know about your audience, the more you can tailor your content, and the more you can turn your niche into a sellable, scalable brand. So get in there, look at those numbers, and let the data drive your way to sold-out shows and a fat paycheck.

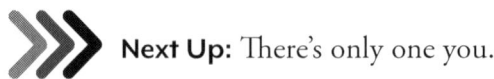 **Next Up:** There's only one you.

Did I say "paycheck?" You've done a lot of work, and you are one element away from cashing out by developing multiple income streams. Everything has been heading to this point—having something to sell. And that something is your unique, quirky comedy brand.

ELEMENT #4: YOUR BRAND

Chapter 16

Your Quirky Brand

• • • • • • • • • • • •

"The more yourself you are, the more original you are."
—James Acaster, comic

• • • • • • • • • • • •

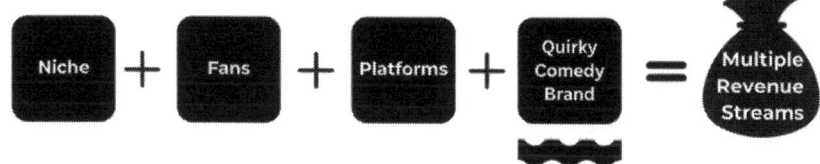

What Makes You Memorable?

You've got your niche. You've found your people. You're posting content. Now comes the fun (and profitable) part: turning all that into a *quirky, memorable brand* that people can't stop talking about—and booking.

Because let's be honest: funny is everywhere. But funny *and* unforgettable? That's rare. That's bankable.

Your Quirky Comedy Brand is how you show up online, on stage, and in your audience's mind. It's the distinct *you-ness*—your voice, perspective, delivery, story, even your props or platforms—that turns followers into fans and gigs into income.

If someone can describe you in one sentence—like "She's that lesbian Southern ex-teacher who jokes about growing up religious," (Fortune Feimster) or "He's that angry guy who rants about the news like he's about to have a stroke" (Lewis Black)—you've got a brand.

There are *three ways* to stand out from the comedy herd and brand yourself like a pro:

1. **Mash up your niches**—find unexpected combinations that make you one of a kind.
2. **Perform in unique places**—From pickup trucks to bathtubs, *weird* sells.
3. **Diversify your delivery**—Don't just talk. Use music, magic, media—whatever makes you pop.

These are the ingredients to build a comedy brand that's not only original but opens doors, earns income, and gets remembered.

 **Next up:** Let's mix and match these ingredients to create *your* unforgettable comedy brand.

ELEMENT #4: YOUR BRAND

—— Chapter 17 ——

Mix and Match Your Niches

• • • • • • • • • • • •

*"Take this time to create your own voice.
It's the most important thing in the world.
Nobody can take that from you."*
—S̄ᴀʀᴀʜ Sɪʟᴠᴇʀᴍᴀɴ

• • • • • • • • • • • •

Case Study: The Truck Driver Tour Guide

You've got a niche—awesome. But how do you *stand out* in it?

Here's the secret: hybrids. Just like dispensaries create new strains of cannabis by blending Sativa and Indica, you can make a brand-new comedy product by mixing your niche with another. Nurse + Burnout. Tech + Drag. Truck Driver + Town Historian. The magic happens in the mash-up.

One comedian I coached—a high-energy, hilarious trucker and father of two—started posting comedy from his delivery truck. He layered in stories about being a dad and a Black man in rural America and eventually gave *funny town tours* of places he passed through. That unique combo? It exploded online. Now he's booked by trucking associations and planning a merch line.

Pro Comics Who've Mastered the Mash-Up:

Bo Burnham

Music + Performance Art + Mental Health Commentary

Bo Burnham started as a teenage YouTube sensation with snarky, satirical songs filmed in his bedroom. But instead of staying in the internet lane, he evolved into something entirely new: a multimedia, emotionally raw, genre-defying artist. His Netflix special *Remarkable Inside*, wasn't just a comedy show—it was a psychological roller coaster filmed during the pandemic, blending original music, lighting design, monologues, and meta commentary on fame, anxiety, and isolation.

Results: A viral hit, Emmy wins, sold-out specials, and a distinct audience who follow him not just for laughs—but for catharsis.

Maria Bamford

Mental Illness + Absurdist Humor + Family Commentary

Maria Bamford doesn't just joke about mental health—she *embodies* it onstage. Diagnosed with bipolar II and OCD, she brings these lived experiences into her comedy, often playing her overbearing mother, her therapist, and even her own inner critic. Her delivery swings from sweet and sincere to surreal and cartoonishly unhinged—all in the same bit. In her Netflix show *Lady Dynamite*, she plays a fictionalized version of herself as she recovers from a psychotic break while trying to rebuild her life and career.

The Mash-Up Magic: By mixing personal mental health struggles, family dynamics, and absurdist character voices, Bamford's brand isn't just funny—it's radically vulnerable and deeply original.

Results: A loyal fanbase, cult-classic TV shows, sold-out storytelling events, and a reputation as a trailblazer in comedy and mental health advocacy.

Kris Andersson (Dixie Longate):
Drag + Tupperware + Solo Theater Show

Kris Andersson took two seemingly unrelated elements—Tupperware and drag—and turned them into a comedy juggernaut. As *Dixie Longate*, a fast-talking Southern belle with a filthy mouth and a plastic container fetish, he created a one-woman show that *doubles* as a real-life Tupperware party. The show, *Dixie's Tupperware* Party, premiered at the NYC Fringe and went on to become an off-Broadway sensation that toured internationally.

The Mash-Up Magic: Andersson combined live theater, direct audience sales, and campy drag into a product that was both performance and commerce.

Results: One of the longest-running solo shows in the U.S., major Tupperware sales commissions, a second show (*Dixie's Never Wear a Tube Top While Riding a Mechanical Bull*), and a cult fanbase who show up ready to buy and laugh.

Exercise #16:
Niche Mashup

---

1. **Mash Up**—Revisit your top 3 niche ideas in Exercise #7: Rate and Rank Them All. Combine them in unexpected ways.
2. **Explore Trends**—What are your niche audiences obsessed with right now? Add that. It could be that you're a therapist who evaluates celebrities online or an accountant dancing to the trendy song of the day.
3. **Test with your Accountability Buddy**—Try mash-ups in conversation or on stage.
4. **Watch Your Metrics**—Your audience will tell you what hits. Double down.

Your Accountability Buddy is not available? Let AI do it for you:

AI Exercise: Mash-Up My Comedy Niches
Prompt to give ChatGPT (or another AI tool):

"I'm a comedian working on developing a unique comedy brand by combining niche topics. My main comedy niche is [INSERT YOUR MAIN NICHE, e.g., 'being a nurse']. I also have experience or interest in [INSERT SECOND NICHE OR TOPICS, e.g., 'mental health,' 'being a parent,' 'gaming,' 'being queer,' or 'living in the South'].

Please give me 10 creative niche mashup ideas that could inspire a unique comedy persona, product, or live show. Each idea should include a short title, a one-sentence concept, and the kind of audience it might attract."

Example Input:
"I'm a comedian. My primary comedy niche is being a public-school teacher. I'm also into sci-fi, single parenting, and being Jewish. Provide me with 10 creative mashup ideas to help me develop a unique comedy brand, along with a one-sentence description of the show I would make based on this mashup of niches."

Here are some examples from my comedy students:

Sambar & Standup
Concept: A brunch stand-up series at Indian restaurants where audiences eat dosas while comedians serve piping hot jokes.
—Tanya Vora

Relapse & Rhythm
Concept: A cabaret-style show blending soulful or hip-hop musical moments with darkly funny stories about addiction, relapse, and cultural identity confusion. —Alana J

Exercise #17:
Use AI to Write Your Brand Title, Description, and Merch Ideas

Coaching Tip:

Create Folders in ChatGPT "Projects"

This way, AI will keep track of all versions of your descriptions, so you don't have to repeat yourself.

Ask AI This:

Brand Building:

"Based on my one, two, or three niches [INSERT THEM], can you suggest potential comedy personas, show titles, description taglines, and types of merch or products that would align with this hybrid comedy brand?"

>
> *"Your audience will tell you what works. Look at your analytics and double down on what's resonating—that's how you build a brand."*
>
> —MEREDITH LYNCH

By mixing and matching your niches, you'll create a one-of-a-kind comedy brand that's not only uniquely yours but also irresistibly sellable.

 **Next Up:** Your mashed-up niches create something uniquely YOU. Now, let's send you out into the world!

ELEMENT #4: YOUR BRAND

—— Chapter 18 ——

Define, Diversify & Deliver

• • • • • • • • • • • •

"Comedy is like music. You have to know your rhythm, but you also have to play with it."
—REGGIE WATTS

• • • • • • • • • • • •

Diversify Your Delivery to Define Your Brand

You've got your niche.

Now, let's talk about the thing that makes you unforgettable and gives you a quirky brand: *how you deliver your material.*

This chapter will help you dial in your delivery style, whether on stage, on screen, or even in the comments section. Because consistency isn't boring—it's branding.

A strong comedy brand doesn't just rely on your unique perspective or story. It also shines through *how* you present that material.

> Your delivery is what makes your comedy pop, stick, and connect.

And when you diversify your performance elements—adding music, movement, characters, visuals, or magic—you don't just stand out—you *become* the standout.

It's about turning your act into a fully expressive version of *you*, tailored for your niche audience, whether you're onstage, online, or somewhere in between.

Performance Elements to Consider

Review this list and check as many skills and talents you might want to incorporate into your act or online to make your brand memorable:

- **Musical Comedy**

  Integrating original songs or parodies that align with your comedic voice can be a great way to deliver jokes in a way that's catchy and memorable.

  Lizzie Cooperman is a Multi-Talented, Multi-Platform Oddball. She's not just a stand-up; she's also a poet, tarot reader, and actress, and she smashes these personas together. That mashup—part mystic, part comic, part performance artist—makes her impossible to pin down, which is her edge.

- **Physical Comedy**

  Use exaggerated gestures, slapstick, or mime to amplify your jokes. Adding a visual layer can make your set more engaging.

  Hannah Einbinder, Co-star of *Hacks*. She sometimes incorporates dance-like physicality and movement into her stand-up routines, giving them a theatrical feel.

- **Impressions and Voices**

  Developing characters, accents, or impressions can make your storytelling more immersive and entertaining.
  - **Melissa Villaseñor**—Known for her expert celebrity impressions on *SNL*.

- **Jay Pharoah**—A master at mimicking voices from Obama to Denzel Washington.
- **Frank Caliendo**—Builds entire comedic bits around his ability to mimic famous voices.

- **Storytelling**

  Expand your storytelling skills with heightened drama or suspense. Make your audience feel like they're part of the narrative.

  Mike Birbiglia blends humor with deeply personal and cinematic storytelling, performing in theaters and on stage.

- **Improvisation and Crowd Work**

  Add improvised segments to your act, such as crowd work or on-the-spot humor, to keep your performance fresh and engaging. Comedians like Jimmy Carr excel at interactive comedy.

  Jeff Ross—The "Roastmaster General," Ross is known for engaging the crowd through sharp, often brutal but hilarious roasting. As of the time of writing, he is performing off-Broadway in his highly acclaimed solo show.

- **Props and Visual Gags**

  Integrate props, costumes, or visual aids to reinforce punchlines.

  Tape Face (Sam Wills). He's a modern classic in the prop, mime, and visual comedy space. He performs with minimal speech, heavy reliance on props, silence, and surreal visual elements.

- **Multimedia Elements**

  With digital screens and social media integration, comedy doesn't have to be just a microphone and a stage anymore.

  Chris Fleming—Blends stand-up, absurdist humor, and heavily produced videos into a unique multimedia comedy experience.

- **Dance or Choreographed Movement**
  If movement fits your style, consider incorporating dance elements for comedic contrast or exaggeration.

  Martin Urbano—Uses awkward, exaggerated dance moves and physicality to enhance his satirical, high-energy comedy.

- **Magical Elements**
  Simple magic tricks with a comedic twist can make your act stand out, as well as other elements such as ventriloquism, clowning, or even performing your act on stilts.

  Justin Willman—Merges sleight-of-hand tricks with observational humor.

Case Study: Justin Willman—Comedy Meets Magic

Justin Willman doesn't just tell jokes—he *disappears* cards and expectations. With his Netflix show "*Magic for Humans*" and a touring stage act, he seamlessly merges sleight of hand, illusions, and comedy into one unforgettable brand.

What sets him apart? He didn't choose between magician and comedian—he became both. That mix helped him stand out, book bigger gigs, and build a loyal fanbase.

Exercise #18: Your Performance Toolkit

Not every performance element will suit your comedic style, and that's okay. The goal is to experiment and find what feels authentic to you and complements your brand.

Start with these steps:

1. **List Your Skills:** Write down any hobbies or skills you've developed (e.g., singing, playing an instrument, acting).

2. **Check out the videos of the comedians listed above for examples.** See who resonates with you and add them as a *secondary Comedy Blueprint.*

3. **Identify Complementary Elements:** Consider which of the performance elements above could integrate seamlessly with your existing material.

4. **Being Different:** Go back to Exercise #11: Find Your Blueprint to Success, where you wrote what you liked and didn't like about your original Blueprint Comic. Which comedy delivery element would make you different from your original Blueprint Comic?

5. **Experiment:** Write or rehearse a short set that incorporates one of these new elements.

6. **Test It Out:** Try the material at an open mic or small show and pay attention to audience reactions.

Final Thoughts: Stand Out by Embracing Your Uniqueness

Diversifying your comedy delivery adds *depth, versatility, and originality* to your brand, enhancing its overall appeal. It makes your act *more engaging, more memorable, and more bookable.*

 **Next Up:** In the next chapter, I'll help you test, tweak, and refine your quirky comedy brand until it's something no one else can replicate. Because building a brand that connects isn't about being perfect—it's about being real, risky, and relentlessly you.

ELEMENT #4: YOUR BRAND

—— Chapter 19 ——

Evolve Through Experimentation

• • • • • • • • • • • • • • •

"The road to success is paved with failures. The more you fail, the better you get. You have to be willing to bomb to figure out who you really are on stage."

— CHRIS ROCK

• • • • • • • • • • • • • • •

The Alchemy of Testing, Tweaking, and Standing Out

When you're prepping for a big event and need the perfect outfit, you try on a parade of options. Most don't fit. Some look great on the hanger but feel like garbage on you. Frustrating, right?

But then—*bam*. You find the outfit that makes you feel unstoppable.

Building your quirky comedy brand is the same. Except instead of just *looking* like a million bucks, you're creating something that could *make* you a million dollars.

The Art of Trial and Error

Creating material and connecting with your niche audience takes grit, patience, and a willingness to bomb spectacularly. Your audience isn't won in a single moment; it's built through consistent engagement and experimentation. Comedy gold isn't mined; it's refined.

Experimenting with Your Quirky Comedy Brand

In earlier chapters, you explored adding:

- Personal stories.
- A secondary niche.
- A unique delivery style.

Now it's time to take all those pieces and play. Test your ideas by experimenting with different combinations. Try the weird thing. Say the risky line. Comedy is the only art form where failure *in public* is part of the process.

Exercise #19: Workshop Your New Brand Elements

- **Buddy System:** Partner with your Accountability Buddy to workshop material. Two minds (and an audience's laugh track) are better than one.

> A former student from my Comedy Workshop told me that 16 years later, eight of them still meet to workshop material (and drink). A writing group beats any book club hands down.

- **Social Media Tryouts:** Post snippets on Instagram or TikTok and ask for feedback. Engagement is your compass.
- **Living Room Laughs:** Host a low-stakes comedy night for friends and get honest feedback in a relaxed setting.

- **Sneaky Open Mic Trials:** Slip new material into your usual set and gauge reactions.
- **The Iteration Loop:** Bomb? Tweak it. Crushed? Refine it. Comedy is a game of reps.

**Coaching Tip:
Commit to You!**

One of my students was killing it with musical parodies at The Comedy Store. Then a fellow comic told her, "Drop the songs—they're a crutch." So, she did. She also eventually quit comedy. Last I heard, she works at Amazon (and not as a Prime comedian).

Moral of the story? Don't take advice that waters down your voice once you find your thing—your edge—double down. The occasional flop is the price of being original.

The Seinfeld/Larry David Commitment

Jerry Seinfeld—before becoming the richest comedian in the world—was just another stand-up in Philly. After a raunchy opener bombed, he stuck to his clean, observational humor. The crowd was cold at first—but he stayed the course and won them over.

Later, when executives wanted *Seinfeld* to be about something, Larry David refused. They even fired a producer who tried to insert moral lessons into the show. Larry took over—and "a show about nothing" became a cultural landmark.

> Find your voice. Then defend it as if your rent depends on it, because it might.

>
> **Coaching Tip:**
> **Say Goodbye to Beloved Jokes**
>
> Some jokes *kill*—but don't fit your brand. That 10-minute oral sex bit? Maybe not ideal for your 8 a.m. corporate gig.
>
> Make a *Farewell Tour List* for material that's hilarious but no longer aligned with your current voice or audience. Let go to level up.

Alchemy in Action

Think of yourself as a comedy alchemist, blending elements until you strike gold. Whether it's new niches, formats, or experimental lighting, your willingness to test and refine will uncover your perfect comedic formula.

Once you find it, *embrace* it. Own it like your perfect outfit. Your audience will tell you it's working, your gut will confirm it, and your brand will become unstoppable.

Exercise #20: Update & Refine Your Brand Description

In this exercise, we will refine the brand description you started creating in Exercise #8: Create a Bio That Fits Your Niche Persona and Exercise #17: Use AI to Write Your Brand Title, Description, and Merch Ideas. Every time you add an element to your show, it changes your description.

Start with this:

"If someone had to describe my comedy in one sentence, what would they say?"

Not sure? Ask your Buddy. Or better yet—ask ChatGPT.

 **Ask AI This:**

"I'm a comedian who wants to find and describe my brand. My most popular social media posts are [DESCRIBE THEM].
My niche is [MASH-UP NICHE].
My audience is [WHO THEY ARE].
In my live show, I talk about [TOPICS].
My delivery is [DEADPAN? HIGH ENERGY? ETC.].
I also use [IMPRESSIONS? MUSIC? DANCE? ETC.].
My style is [CLEAN, DARK, SASSY, RAW, ETC.].
Based on this, give me five one-sentence brand descriptions I could use in a bio or pitch."

Here are some examples from my students:

From Tanya Vora: "My comedy bridges cultures and identities—offering a safe, funny place for anyone who's ever felt like too much, too brown, or too weird to belong."

From Shelby Lane: "Where medicine meets mayhem—I deliver clean, dark laughs about life as a doctor in the toughest neighborhoods, using dance and storytelling to expose the wild side of healthcare."

From Me: "Judy Carter turns problems into punchlines—using clean, edgy humor, music, and magic to show audiences that laughter is a superpower."

Exercise #21:
Add Your USP

What's a USP—and why does it matter?

USP = Unique Selling Proposition. It answers one big question: *Why you?*

For comedians, your USP is the *combo meal* of your voice, niche, delivery style, and POV.

- Are you the brutally honest mom who makes PTA jokes feel like a threat?
- The neurodivergent comic who turns overstimulation into punchlines?
- The ex-nurse who roasts hospital chaos with surgical precision?

That's your USP. And when you claim it, your comedy becomes more than funny—it becomes *marketable*.

Ask AI This: USP Brand Statement

"Now that you know my brand—[INSERT BRAND DESCRIPTION FROM PREVIOUS EXERCISE]—add a strong USP statement to it."

Print out your final brand description and USP. Tape it to your wall. Tattoo it on your frontal lobe. Let it guide every set, every post, every pitch. In fact, let AI write your bio for each social media platform.

This is what it came up with for me:

For my website:

"Judy Carter turns problems into punchlines—using clean, edgy humor, music, and even magic to show audiences that laughter is a superpower—transforming any event into an unforgettable, interactive experience of insight and hilarity."

Ask AI This: Update Your Socials

Let AI write your bio for each social media platform.

"Now that you know my brand and I have a strong USP statement, please rewrite my social media bio for INSERT CURRENT SOCIAL MEDIA PLATFORMS with current word limitations."

This is what it came up for me.

TikTok Bio:

🎤 Comedian + Speaker turning stress into stand-up.
💥 Laughter = your superpower.

Instagram Bio:

🎤 Clean, edgy comedian + speaker turning stress into stand-up.
💥 Laughter is a superpower—follow for laughs + life hacks.

 **Next Up:** Get ready to turn your brand into a bankable product—one that creates multiple income streams and a comedy business that works *even when you're not on stage*.

ELEMENT #5: MULTIPLE REVENUE STREAMS

—— Chapter 20 ——

Create Multiple Comedy Revenue Streams

• • • • • • • • • • • • •

"People say money can't buy happiness, but I say if you have enough money, you can have a key made."

—Joan Rivers

• • • • • • • • • • • • •

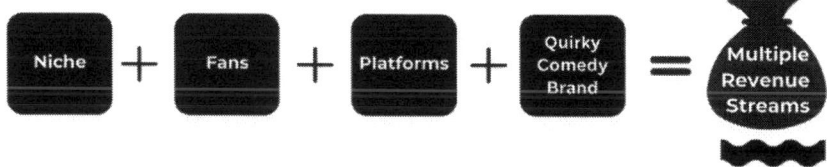

For Everyone Who *Did* the Work—Congratulations

If you skipped ahead thinking you could jump straight to the money bag without doing the work of finding your niche, I hate to break it to you, but you're trying to fry an egg without turning on the stove. Don't even think about DM'ing me to ask, "Why isn't this working?" if you haven't laid the groundwork BEFORE trying to create the revenue streams. No niche? No cash flow.

> You're no longer just "trying to be funny."
> You're ready to get paid for it.

What You've Built So Far

If you've done the work so far, then you're no longer just "trying comedy."

You've built the foundation of a full-blown comedy business.

Let's recap:

- You've nailed your niche—you know exactly who you're talking to.
- You've built a connection with your fans—they're commenting, sharing, laughing.
- You've tested content on the right platforms—and figured out what works.
- You've crafted a quirky, unforgettable brand that makes you stand out in a sea of sameness.

> "The setup is over. Now comes the punchline and the paycheck."

That, my friend, is the *Comedy Cash Flow Formula*.

And now? You're only 20 feet from striking comedy gold—creating multiple income streams.

In this section, we'll break down exactly *what comedy revenue streams are*—and why they're your ticket out of the one-gig-at-a-time grind.

You'll learn:

- Why you *don't* need a Netflix special to make real money
- What "streams" actually look like for stand-up comics, creators, and character-based weirdos like you

- How to start *one stream right now* that could grow into a six-figure river by creating comedy products
- And the difference between money from working gigs (contract-based) versus owning your own IP (Intellectual Property), where you get "money while you sleep."

Next Up: In the next chapter, we'll break down the two types of comedy income—contract-based and ownership-based—because understanding the difference is key to structuring your comedy business for long-term income security.

You're not just chasing laughs anymore.

You're building something that pays beyond the stage.

ELEMENT #5: MULTIPLE REVENUE STREAMS

— Chapter 21 —

Fast Cash vs. Forever Cash

• • • • • • • • • • • • •

"You have to find ways to create income while you sleep. If the only money you make is from the work you physically do, you'll never create wealth."
—STEVE HARVEY

• • • • • • • • • • • • •

Stop Chasing Gigs. Start Owning Sh*t.

You want comedy to do more than just pay your bills.

You want it to buy you freedom. Options. Security.

This chapter is your gateway to that future.

It's simple: Own shit rather than being owned by others.

Most comics are stuck on the gig treadmill: hustle, perform, get paid, repeat.

But if you stop moving? The money stops, too.

That's *Fast Cash*.

This chapter is about stepping off the hamster wheel and building what every working comedian needs: *a system that pays you while you sleep.*

Let's talk about the *two lanes of comedy money*.

Coaching Tip:
Don't get overwhelmed by this chapter
You don't have to *do* anything right now. This information is designed to help you understand how money works, so your future self can make the most of it.

1. Contract-Based Gigs: Fast, Fleeting, and Familiar

These are the gigs you already know:

- Stand-up shows
- Acting roles
- Voiceovers
- Hosting events
- Writing jokes for someone else

They're fast money gigs. You get paid *once*. No ownership. No royalties.

You're the hired talent. Someone else owns the product. And it's a sure-fire recipe for burnout. I know because I've been there. I was on the road working clubs 46 weeks a year. Crushing it onstage. Broke by summer. Every time I stopped moving? The money stopped too. I was like a shark—constantly having to swim to stay alive.

There's another way. There are "gigs" where freedom lives. "Gigs" that create ownership-based income and products you can sell, such as:

- A book
- A comedy special
- A course
- A podcast
- A character

- Merchandise
- A branded show

Owning IP is how comedians build real wealth.

Not by gigging harder, but by owning their intellectual property (IP) and leveraging it.

In *The New Comedy Bible*, I ask beginning comics, "When will you consider yourself successful?" The most common answer? "When I have a million dollars."

That's not success.

Success isn't how much you have in the bank—it's how much comes in every month, *whether you're working or not.*

>  *"I don't want to be in a position where I'm just the talent. I want to own. I want to create. I want to produce."*
> —**KEVIN HART, MULTIPLE INTERVIEWS**

You're not just the act—you're the asset. Own what you sell.

Financial freedom doesn't come from one big windfall. (Let's be honest, by the time a writer sells a screenplay, they've racked up three years of debt writing it.) It comes from a mix of steady gigs and owned assets that continue to generate income for you.

Here's how pros do it:

- **Comedy Clubs/Production Companies**—Joe Rogan co-owns Comedy Mothership; Adam Sandler built Happy Madison Productions.
- **Talent Management/Production Deals**—Kevin Hart's Hartbeat Productions and Laugh Out Loud Network allow him to own a piece of other comics' work.

- **Label or Studio**—Hannibal Buress and Tig Notaro release albums through their own imprints.
- **Tour Management**—Produce and promote your own tours, like Oddball, Netflix Is a Joke, or Zarna Garg's self-produced tour.
- **Owning Real Estate**—Turn the first of the month into the day you get paid rent, not the day you pay it.

Case Study: How I Made 10x More Without a Publisher

"When the gatekeepers stop answering your calls, build your own damn gate."

I've published seven books with major publishers. I've done the dance—book proposals, advances, editorial notes from people who don't know comedy, and waiting a year (or more) to see my book in print. And when it does come out, it's up to me to promote it. I watch as the bulk of my advance is spent on marketing that I pay for, only to receive 10% of the royalties. One of those books became a *bestseller*—and you'd think the publisher would be thrilled to publish my next one. But when I pitched the follow-up? *Crickets*. They ghosted me. So I self-published. Yes, I had to put up my own money for editing, design, and formatting. No, I didn't get a $100,000 advance. But here's what I *did* get:

- Creative control.
- Direct access to my audience.
- And the full royalty rate.

Because I'm known in a *niche*—comedians—I had a direct line to the people who wanted the book. And guess what? *My self-published book has earned ten times what I earned from my traditionally published ones.*

The truth?

The publishing industry isn't about empowering authors.

It's about protecting their bottom line.

Just like comedy bookers, streaming platforms, and networks.

Don't wait for someone to "pick you." Pick yourself.

> Own your content. Own your future.

 **Coaching Tip:
Keep Calm & Carry On**

Reminder: Don't get overwhelmed.

This chapter isn't about doing something today—it's about understanding what's possible tomorrow. Knowledge is power, and the more you know how ownership works, the more control (and cash flow) you'll eventually have and the less overwhelmed you will feel.

Case Studies in Ownership-Based Brilliance

Sam Morril

Instead of waiting for Netflix to call, Sam put his specials on YouTube. Millions of views → More fans → More ticket sales → More ownership. Netflix came later—on his terms.

Andrew Schulz

Turned down by networks, he self-released *4:4:1* and *Infamous* and went on to make millions. He didn't just release a special—he launched a comedy product like an entrepreneur.

The Tyler Perry Billion-Dollar Model

Tyler Perry didn't wait for Hollywood. He began with live shows catering to his niche: faith-based, church-going Black audiences.

He wrote, produced, and sold DVDs of his Madea plays directly to his fans.

When Lionsgate came knocking, he kept ownership.

His movies? Over $1 billion at the box office. Why?

He owned the rights.

Coaching Tip:
Why You Need Both

Let's be clear—contract gigs pay the rent, and it's where you develop your material.

But if you're not building something you own, you're just a talented freelancer.

Your gigs should fund your assets.
Use the fast cash to build your forever cash.

Gigs = Cash Now
Ownership = Cash Forever

Case in Point: Louis C.K.'s Million-Dollar Bounce Back

In 2017, Louis C.K. was "canceled" following a 2017 exposé in The *New York Times* that detailed his history of sexual misconduct, which he admitted. He lost everything—Netflix, FX, HBO, and his team.

But he didn't go broke. Why?

He emulated George Carlin who was one of the **earliest major stand-up comics to deliberately treat his comedy as owned intellectual property** and build a **long-term income-producing catalog** from on a major scale.

Live at the Beacon Theater made $1M in 12 days—sold from his own site.

He runs his own store. Owns his list. Owns his content.

Ownership kept him in the game.

> **Ownership protects against censorship**
>
> At the time of writing, the Trump Administration is reportedly considering firing comedians such as Stephen Colbert and Jimmy Kimmel for jokes about speaking truth to power. But, their solution? Own their own distribution of their material. In the end, it's the way to go.

Exercise #22: Comedy Income Reality Check

Let's get honest about where your money is coming from—and where it could come from next.

Step #1: Reality Check

Look over the two lists below.

- ☑ Check what you've done.
- ◯ Circle what you're currently doing.
- ☆ Star what you'd like to try.

A. Contract-Based (Active Work)

_____ Stand-up shows

_____ Keynote speaking

_____ Acting roles

_____ Hosting/Emceeing

_____ Teaching comedy or writing

_____ Scriptwriting for others

_____ Joke writing for brands or comics

_____ Consulting (humor, branding)

_____ One-person shows or tours.

_____ Podcast or panel guesting

_____ Staff writing gigs

_____ Specialty event gigs (roasts, weddings)

B. Ownership-Based (Passive or Scalable Income)

_____ Books (memoirs, humor, how-to)

_____ Comedy specials (streaming or downloads)

_____ Podcasts (with ads or sponsors)

_____ Merch (t-shirts, mugs, digital art)

_____ Monetized content (YouTube, TikTok)

_____ Syndication or rerun royalties

_____ Licensing jokes or personas

_____ Patreon or subscription models

_____ Selling scripts or treatments

_____ Musical comedy royalties

_____ Comedy games or apps

_____ Online courses or e-books

_____ Affiliate marketing

> An affiliate promotes a company's product or service using a unique, trackable link. When someone clicks it and makes a purchase (even a BBQ grill or microphone), you earn a small cut.
>
> I've set up Amazon affiliate links for my books—so for 48 hours after someone buys one, any other items they purchase on Amazon earn me a commission.

Step #2: Turn a Gig Into a Gold Mine

Pick one gig from your contract list and ask:

"How can I turn this into something I own?"

Example: A charity books you for a fundraiser. You crush it. Instead of just saying, "Thanks for the gig," say, "Want help booking the next one?" *Boom*—you curate the lineup, produce the show, and pocket an agent's cut.

That's ownership thinking.

You're not just doing gigs—you're building a money machine.

Step #3: Turn Your Gig Into an Opportunity

 Let **AI** be your brainstorming buddy. Copy, paste, and fill in the blanks:

Prompt:
"I've been doing [INSERT GIG] for [X years/months].

Based on that, what comedy product could I own or scale?
Give me three ideas I could turn into recurring income (like a live show, course, book, podcast, special, merch, or digital series).
Also, what's the first step to start building it?"

Example Prompt:
"I've been performing stand-up comedy for eight years.
Based on that, what comedy product could I own or scale?
Give me three ideas for recurring income and the first step for each."

Example AI Results (Student: Bob Siegel, Boomer comic):

- **Ownership Product:** Launch a "Boomer-approved" merch line or digital download (easy win).
- **Contract Gig:** Produce a Boomer Grandpa storytelling show or class (locals will eat it up).
- **Video Content:** Start a weekly Boomer Reacts series—grows your audience and feeds your other gigs.

Step #4: Design Your Ultimate Vision

By now, you've seen the power of ownership. Perhaps AI has given you ideas that feel exciting—or overwhelming. That's okay. You're exploring what's possible.

Now it's time to define *your* vision. Imagine your future where your gigs feed your freedom. Where some money comes from the stage, and some arrives while you're sleeping.

Write for 10 minutes:

Describe what your ideal comedy career looks like five years from now.

- What does your week look like?
- How many income streams do you have?
- What products, shows, or properties do you own?
- What kind of work brings you joy—and what no longer drains you?

Your vision isn't about being "realistic." It's about being *intentional*. Put this vision of your career somewhere you can see it every day.

Step #5: Invest in Your Future—and Own It

Creating intellectual property means taking ownership of your comedy—and ownership always requires investment. You can't own your future if you're not willing to invest in it.

Start small, but start now. Open a "Comedy Ownership Fund"—even if you can only set aside $5 a week. It's not the amount that matters; it's the intention. Each deposit is a declaration to the universe: "*I believe in my talent. I believe in my future.*"

Every product you create—a show, a podcast, a course—will need something tangible to back it up: a domain name, editing software, design tools, or maybe just coffee to keep you writing. Those small investments build the foundation of your creative empire.

Ownership isn't about waiting for a network, an agent, or a miracle. It's about saying, "This is my vision, my show, my product—and I'm willing to put something behind it."

 **Next Up:** Your First New Stream

Dreaming is excellent—but now, we'll take your first small step toward building one of those streams.

ELEMENT #5: MULTIPLE REVENUE STREAMS

—— Chapter 22 ——

Start a Stream, Grow a River

• • • • • • • • • • • •

*"Your comedy isn't just a show—it's an ecosystem:
A creek of courage, a stream of jokes, and before you
know it, you're swimming in the Ocean of Opportunity."*
—JUDY CARTER

• • • • • • • • • • • •

Start Small. Build Big. Own Everything.

Starter Comedy Streams

Ultimately, if you are a performing comedian, you'll want to create a *live 60-minute comedy show as your tentpole product, one that you own and control.* But here we will begin with a starter stream that gets your comedy moving and connects you to your niche. Maybe it's a piece of merchandise, such as one of your killer jokes that you turn into a sticker, or you conduct a mini comedy workshop at your company that leads to more workshops, and then you emcee their awards banquet.

Whatever you choose here, it's just a *bridge* to the bigger product—your live comedy show you can sell, tour, and scale. But that's the next chapter in this book. But for now? You're jumpstarting momentum. Think of this as a warm-up sprint—*not a marathon.*

Because odds are:
> You've already got a stream that's flowing.
> You just haven't recognized it as money, or it's something already generating income, but you haven't linked it to your comedy career—yet.

The Law of Comedy Momentum

> **Think Big, Start Small**
>
> Even Kevin Hart didn't launch an empire overnight. He started selling sneakers. That turned into material. That turned into a stand-up. That turned into specials. That turned into movies, brand deals, and an entire fitness line.

> *Your first stream doesn't need to go viral.*
> It just needs to *flow*.

Every big money maker starts small.

> **When you treat every show, every post, and every product like it could lead to the next thing, it often will.**

- A short video goes viral → You sell shirts with the catchphrase.
- A corporate gig kills → They ask if you facilitate trainings.
- Your Zoom storytelling workshop gets love → You pitch it to a podcast network.
- A live show with a niche theme → Attracts sponsors from that industry.

You don't need to invent new material constantly.

You just need to connect what you already have to the next possible opportunity. You also need to spot opportunities.

One-person show → Corporate speaking gigs

A comic created a solo show about surviving divorce. After one emotional performance, a therapist in the audience asked her to speak at a women's retreat. That retreat led to two more events. That show now makes more as a "healing keynote" than it ever did in clubs.

> Every gig is a pitch. Every laugh is a lead. Every piece of content is a clue.

TikTok series → Book deal → Product line

A funny nurse on TikTok did a video about "How nurses pretend to care when they're exhausted." It blew up. She made a mug. Then merch. Then a book. Now she's headlining a nursing cruise.

Teaching stand-up → Corporate consulting

A PR firm asked a comedian who ran open-mic workshops for beginners if she could coach their executives to "be more human on stage." Now she teaches humor in business and earns four times her old club rate. (Oh, wait, that's me!)

The Free to Fee Pipeline

To get your momentum going, let's take a lesson from an unexpected group of business geniuses—*drug dealers*.

Their business model is flawless: Give out free samples, get people hooked, and have them coming back with cash and desperation in their eyes.

I once did the same thing—minus the meth.

I volunteered to teach a free comedy workshop at a National Speakers Association meeting. I pulled up a few speakers and made them funnier in front of the group. Suddenly, everyone wanted me to polish their speech. I came home with $30,000 from private consultations.

See? *Free* can lead to *fee*, and without needing a criminal record.

Success story: "Pay What You Can"

Comedian **Maria Bamford** built fan loyalty by offering "Pay What You Can" tickets to her live shows. It turns out that people paid *more* than expected—proving that generosity can be addictive too.

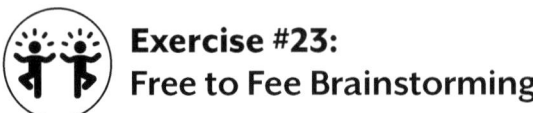

Exercise #23: Free to Fee Brainstorming

Pick one of these ideas and do it! Take action.

1. Personalized Video Shoutouts

Use *Cameo, ShoutOut,* or *Memmo* to record funny birthday or roast messages based on your niche. Sure, you might not be a celebrity. Yet, by doing a "Nurse's Rap" or a funny, happy birthday rant, plumbers can get you work, especially if you promote it at work or to your niche-specific association, club, or online. Got a real funny one? Take an Instagram ad out to boost it.

   $25 – $100 each

2. Fiverr Comedy Gigs

Offer joke writing, roast scripts, or punch-ups for speeches and bios. Most speakers are boring and can surely use you. You can start offering coaching and punch-ups for free at your job and watch how the word gets around. I submitted jokes to a local politician. He won. Next thing I knew, he was paying me and recommending me to write material for the Senator of California. Soon, I was delivering a humorous keynote address to the staff of the US Senate. Start your stream!!!

   $50 – $200/project
   Sample gig: "I'll add five custom jokes to your presentation."

3. Merch That Moves

Create t-shirts, mugs, or stickers with your punchlines on *Printful, Bonfire,* or *Redbubble.*

$5 – $20 profit/item

Think: "Laugh Like a Nurse," "Teaching: The Original Reality Show." If they are hilarious, when you bring them to work, everyone will ask you, "Where did you get them?" Give them your QR code and cha-ching!

>  **Coaching Tip:**
> **Pay What You Can**
>
> Diana Hong took her top one-liner and turned it into stickers for just five cents each. After her show, she provides them to her audience for free. Most people pay her $20.

4. Volunteer to speak, perform, or do a workshop for free

One of my students was a greeter at Banana Republic. She created a funny set about customer service and volunteered to speak at a meeting. Next thing you know, she was speaking for money at their National Meeting.

5. Write for other comics

You are already at a comedy club. Watch other comics and add tags to their material for free, and when you see them again, ask them, "Did it work?" When they say, "Yes!" now tell them your rates. You're like a drug dealer giving them a sample, knowing they liked the high of getting a laugh and will now pay for it.

6. Comedy-Themed Events

Host comedy trivia nights for your pickleball club, comedy brunches for your coworkers, or a comedy show for your charity.

$10 – $20 tickets or door split

Partner with bars or cafés—they love bringing in new customers.

Double Down on What's Already Working

To start building more money streams, ask, "*Where am I already getting paid or getting attention?*"

So you might be asking now, "But Judy, when do I quit my day job and score big as a comic?"

Rather than thinking of your day job as something to *quit*, think about expanding that stream of money into a larger comedy stream. Don't lose it—use it. Many of you have already built your niche on it.

A career in comedy and multiple income streams isn't this *or* that— it's this *and* that. Meaning—it's your day job, writing for other comics, driving Uber, and producing your show. Sorry, folks—that's the reality of the gig economy now.

> A career in comedy and multiple income streams isn't this *or* that—it's this *and* that.

From Uber to Stardom

How did Jimmy Shin go from Uber driver to producing comedy shows that he starred in? He made his Uber passengers laugh so much while driving them that when he invited them to his shows, they actually came. Now he has a superpower—filling seats. Soon, he packed out The Comedy Store in Hollywood, producing his own shows monthly. That became *The ShinDig Show*, which attracted comedy celebrities who wanted to try out new material to a packed house. He now produces his own comedy empire. All from a day job that many comics are too ashamed even to admit having.

Exercise #24:
Turn Your Day Job into a Comedy Gig

> "You're not just creating gigs.
> You're building momentum."

Here's the magic rule of comedy income:
> *Every stream creates more streams—even your day job.*

- A teacher could pitch a humorous keynote to other educators
- A therapist could create a "funny self-help" show or TikTok series
- A customer service rep could create a storytelling workshop on "How to Deal with Jerks—Using Humor."
- A funny nurse could write material for Nurse Blake or create a parody med training series.

This is where the real fun begins—not just making money, but watching one opportunity spill into the next. That's how your comedy transforms from a *hustle* into a *flow*.

 **Ask AI This:**

I would like to expand my current role into a comedy-related opportunity.

My day job is: [insert your current job or primary source of income].

My comedy niche or area of humor is: [insert your niche—teaching, healthcare, parenting, corporate life, etc.].

My comedy talent is: [insert what you do best—stand-up, storytelling, sketch, musical comedy, improv, impressions, writing, etc.].

Based on this information, please provide me **with five creative ways** to turn my current job or field into a comedy income stream—such as live performances, online content, a humorous book, a workshop, or something entirely unexpected.

Include ideas for titles or themes that would attract my specific audience.

Example: "Southern Mom Who Sells Jewelry"

Day Job: Sells jewelry at home parties and online
Comedy Niche: Southern mom life, family chaos, small-town living
Comedy Talent: Storytelling and singing
Example:
Live Show—"Bless Your Bling: Tales of a Southern Mom Hustler"

A one-woman comedy show mixing heartfelt stories and funny songs about balancing motherhood, mascara, and multi-level marketing. Perform at women's events, jewelry conventions, and comedy clubs.

Ownership Product: Record it as a special or create a downloadable "Ladies Night In" virtual version.

Think *Leanne Morgan: I'm Every Woman*—in her fifties, she turned everyday Southern mom life into a Netflix special and a national tour. You can do the same with your story.

Why This Matters

Your next big opportunity is hiding inside what you already do.

That's your *gold mine*.

Once you start blending what pays your bills with what makes people laugh, your comedy starts working for you.

 **Next Up:** Your Tentpole Product

Now that you've identified how your existing work and skills can expand into new income streams, it's time to turn one of those ideas into something tangible—*a live one-hour show built specifically for your niche.*

Your live show will be your *tentpole product*—the signature performance that anchors your brand, fuels your marketing, and generates spin-off opportunities into books, workshops, courses, and merchandise.

In the next chapter, we'll start building that show—step by step—to make it the *comedy product that launches your comedy career.*

ELEMENT #5: MULTIPLE REVENUE STREAMS

— Chapter 23 —

Produce the Show That Builds Everything

"Don't just perform. Produce."
—Judy Carter

Your Signature Show Starts Here

You've chosen your starter streams. Maybe it's a podcast. A workshop. A series of short social media videos. Some merch. Or joke writing for others.

If you've been thinking, "Wait—should I have built a live show instead?"—you're right on schedule.

That starter stream was your test balloon. It helped you:

- Bring in some cash
- Get in front of your niche
- See what sticks
- Build early traction and confidence

Now it's time to build your main product. Your live show is the product that ties everything together. It becomes:

- Your most bookable and profitable offering
- The home for your best material
- The experience that builds your fanbase
- The centerpiece for your merch, podcast, coaching, and future products

It's not just a set. It's your brand in action. And who is going to produce it? You.

"But Judy—if this is our career center piece—why didn't we start with this?"

Because you had to develop it from your niche, understand your audience, connect on social media, build your quirky comedy brand, and start making money with small jobs. Now, you are ready.

In this chapter, you'll learn how to take everything you've been developing—your niche, your material, your message—and shape it into a product you own, promote, and monetize.

That product?

Your Live Comedy Show.

If you've mostly been a guest on other people's stages, following their rules and restrictions, it's time to flip the script. You're not just a performer anymore—you're the headliner and producer of your own branded show.

This chapter is your next big step: turning everything you've developed in the previous exercises into a signature comedy product that reflects your unique brand, voice, and niche.

This show becomes the centerpiece of your comedy brand, the product that fuels your other products: merch, workshops, digital content, tours, books, festival submissions, courses, ticketed livestreams, and more. It's the product that creates other products. And the best part? You already have the raw materials.

>  **Coaching Tip:**
> **Hybrid as a Writer/Performer**
>
> Almost every successful late-night comic was a stand-up first—**Conan O'Brien, Amber Ruffin, Seth Meyers, Colin Jost, Sarah Silverman, Wanda Sykes**, etc. Being both a writer and performer creates cross-training: you understand how to write for performance, not just for paper.

What Counts as a Comedy Product?

Before we dig into your show, let's define what "product" means.

Here are a few comedy products:

- A one-person show
- A niche-focused stand-up hour
- A storytelling solo show
- A hilarious and inspiring keynote
- A recurring character or interactive game show
- A script, podcast, workshop, keynote, merch line, or book

Even your TikTok series is a product if you treat it like one.

But your *live comedy show* is the centerpiece. It brings your audience together in one place—*live, in person, or online*—and positions you as a pro with a one-of-a-kind brand and a compelling message tailored to your niche.

Why Your Live Show Is Your Most Powerful Product

A live show is more than just a set. It can be:

- Branded and titled: "Spice, Laughs & Latin Flavor," "The Stoner Comedy Jam," "Confessions of a Funny Nurse."
- Booked at various venues: comedy clubs, theaters, corporate events, festivals, and fundraisers.

- Recorded and monetized: digital downloads, livestreams, specials
- Promote your merch: books, coaching, or your next gig
- Repurposed for: TEDx Talks, podcasts, series pitches, courses, keynote speeches

Whether you've made a name through clubs, viral videos, social media clips, acting, or writing—all roads can (and should) lead to a show you own. A show that reflects your brand. A show that's a product.

Your self-produced live show is how you stop chasing random gigs—and start touring a show you *own*.

Step #1: What's My Show?

So, what exactly is this "product" you're going to create, own, and sell?

It's a branded, themed, *niche-savvy show* that plays to your strengths, speaks to your people, and reflects your point of view. It could be a one-person storytelling show, a high-energy themed hour, a character piece, a game show, a multimedia spectacle, or an interactive improv night. Whatever it is—it's yours.

And here's the good news: You've already been building it in this book.

Remember the brand description from Exercises #20: Update & Refine Your Brand Description and #21: Add Your USP—with the tagline that captured your vibe? That's the foundation of your show. Stepping into the show you create is the moment we shift from hustling for spots . . . to building something that fills rooms, sells tickets, and creates lasting income.

Your show should reflect:

- Your niche
- Your quirky brand
- Your funniest material
- What your audience already loves
- Your message

You're not starting from scratch—you're assembling what you've already written, testing it out on social media, and performing in a way that's *cohesive, branded, and sellable.*

Step #2: Think in 15-Minute Chunks

Don't write an hour—*build four 15-minute blocks*:

    1. Opening—Hook them and introduce your vibe
    2. Core Material—Dive into your niche, tell stories, go deeper
    3. Audience Connection—Interaction, emotional turn, or live improv
    4. Closer—High-impact jokes, callback, standing ovation moment

Yes—your goal is to create an *hour-long show.*

I know. That might sound like climbing Everest in Crocs. But stay with me.

If you break it down into 15-minute chunks—four distinct sections that each connect to your brand and niche—it becomes much more manageable. Think of it like building a house: You're not building the whole thing at once. First, you lay a foundation. Then frame a room. Then another. Before long, you've got something solid, something you can live in—or in your case, *perform in.*

Case Studies: Comics Who Built It and Sold It

From Stand-Up to the Golden Globes

Let's talk about Scottish comedian Richard Gadd. He turned a stand-up set into a one-person show that changed his career. *Monkey See Monkey Do*, which tackled sexual assault and trauma, was performed while he ran on a treadmill at the Edinburgh Festival. It was raw, real, and unforgettable—and it won the Edinburgh Comedy Award in 2016.

But that was just the beginning. Gadd adapted his story into the Netflix miniseries *Baby Reindeer,* which premiered in 2024 and garnered widespread acclaim, winning six Emmys and two Golden Globes. It all started with a live comedy product. His story. His performance. His terms.

Your live show might not land you on Netflix—or maybe it will—but it can become the foundation of a brand, a fan base, and a suite of comedy products you own.

How Bridget Everett Went from Cabaret Gigs to HBO Star

Bridget Everett started her comedy career not in clubs, but in *downtown New York City cabaret bars*, where she performed outrageous, fearless musical comedy braless that was part stand-up, part singing, part wild audience interaction—talk about a quirky comedy brand!

Her unique voice caught the attention of Amy Schumer, leading to roles in *Inside Amy Schumer* and *Trainwreck*. But the big win? HBO's *Somebody Somewhere*—a heartfelt series based on her life in Kansas.

It all started with *owning her voice onstage*. Her show became her brand. Her brand became a product. That product became a series.

> Now ask yourself: What's your version of that show? What live act, story, or idea could you own—and grow into something bigger than a gig?

Exercise #25:
The Product Is YOU!

Follow these steps to mine your material, shape your format, and walk away with a show you can test, pitch, and promote.

Step #1: Mine Your Previous Work

Go back through the earlier exercises in this book and gather clues from what you've already built. Look closely at:
- Your niche discovery (Exercise #7: Rate and Rank Them All)
- Your branded tagline (Exercise #20: Update & Refine Your Brand Description)

- The material that clicked with your audience (Exercise #13: Writing Platform-Specific Comedy Material for Your Niche Audience)
- Your brainstormed show titles and potential product list (Exercise #17: Use AI to Write Your Brand Title, Description, and Merch Ideas)
- And your "Why?" (Exercise #1: Discover Your "Why")

These pieces are the puzzle. Time to start putting them together and step into your Comedy Career Vision from Exercise #2.

Step #2: Define Your Message

If you have been using ChatGPT throughout this book, AI now knows you better than your mom. If you haven't been saving your material using ChatGPT as suggested in "How to Use This Book," then upload your strongest material (clips, bits, or text) to an AI tool and ask:

AI Prompt:

"What message does my comedy convey to my niche audience?"

Use the response to refine your show's focus.

Example result from AI:

"Your comedy message is about empowerment through humor, breaking stereotypes, and finding the universal truth in the chaos of being a woman. You mix outrageousness with sharp observations, giving a raw, unfiltered take on the struggles and triumphs of women across generations."

What that really means:

- Own your flaws, laugh at the madness, and take no BS.
- Aging, relationships, and self-worth aren't off-limits—they're comedy gold.
- Humor is a superpower, and you wield it to connect, challenge, and uplift.

Action Step: Revisit your material. Tighten it up to support this core message.

Step #3: Explore Your Show Format

What form does your show take?

Pull from your work in the Query Brand and Niche chapters—especially the "mashup" exercises and Exercise #17: Use AI to Write Your Brand Title, Description, and Merch Idea. Also, look at Exercise #18: Your Performance Toolkit

This is where you envision your show coming to life.

Answer these:

- Is it a solo or a guest comic?
- Does it involve audience interaction?
- Is it traditional stand-up, a storytelling night, a theatrical experience, or a hybrid?

Examples:

Julie Golden's *The Big D*: A dating game show for divorced singles. She opens with stand-up, features comics as matchmakers, and hosts 12 real singles. Now backed by sponsors and attracting TV interest.

Set List: Stand-Up Without a Net (by Paul Provenza & Troy Conrad): Comics improvise sets from surprise prompts on screen. Started locally. It was adapted into a TV series and became an international hit.

Elizabeth Swaney's *Snark Tank*: A Shark Tank-style roast show where comics judge real startup pitches. A brilliant comedy/tech mashup.

Your Turn—Describe Your Format:

- Solo storytelling?
- Stand-up with a twist?

- A recurring character?
- Musical parody show?
- Half-hour themed set with Q&A?
- Full-blown audience-participation experience?

Get specific. Your live show is your *product prototype*.

Step #4: Give Your Show a Name & Description

You've got the message, format, and structure. Now let's wrap it in a killer package. Your show needs a name that *pops*—and a description that sells. It's now time to really name and describe your show.

Let AI help.

 **AI Prompt: Name & Describe My Comedy Show**

I'm creating a live comedy show. Here are the details:

- Niche/audience: [insert niche]
- Tone/brand: [funny, raw, absurd, empowering, raunchy, uplifting, etc.]
- Format: [solo, hosted show, character-driven, game show, storytelling, musical]
- Other people in the show: [solo, guest comics, audience participation]
- Message or theme: [single parenting, queer joy, tech burnout, divorce, etc.]
- Venue or setting: [clubs, Zoom, festivals, corporate events, theaters]

Based on that, as well as all the information you've gathered from me from other exercises, give me:

1. 5 compelling show titles
2. A 2 – 3 sentence show description I can use for flyers, websites, or pitches. Make it reflect my comedy brand and niche. It should sound exciting, unique, and bookable.

By the end of this exercise, you should walk away with:

- A clear comedy message
- A defined show format
- A compelling title and pitch
- And most importantly, a show that feels like YOU.

Now you're not just performing—you're producing. And producers get paid. Your work ahead is to workshop it, sharpen it, and then launch it.

Workshop Your Show

Don't wait until your show is perfect; rather, workshop it by breaking it into 15-minute sections and *performing it regularly*. Workshopping it in front of real people who already like your material online is also beneficial, as you will learn what works and what doesn't. You're not building the whole house in one night. You're stress-testing one room at a time.

Book a Venue

Comedy Club Side Rooms

Many comedy clubs have smaller showrooms with 20 to 40 seats—perfect for workshopping. These are often "four-walled" setups, where you keep ticket sales and the venue profits from food and drink. While this isn't about making money yet, this setup can grow into a win-win as your product improves.

> **The Comedy Store**
>
> Comedy Store CFO Bob Wheeler notes, "The most financially successful comics aren't always the ones with the biggest credits. They're the ones who produce shows and fill seats regularly."

Think Outside the Comedy Club

Think laundromats, bookstores, community centers, plant shops, outdoor markets, or pet rescue centers. The venue itself can become an integral part of the show's identity, making it both memorable and *Instagrammable*. I saw Ali Wong perform her comedy at the Pleasure Chest in Hollywood, next to dildos. It was the perfect place as it went right in line with her sex jokes.

> **Stand Up for Pets Comedy Show**
>
> At The Annenberg PetSpace, Caitlin Benson created a comedy night where attendees could adopt rescue animals while enjoying stand-up. The event, sponsored by alcohol brands, featured headliners and raised money for animal shelters. Unique? Yes. Memorable? 100%.

Collaborate and Share Costs

If you're just getting started, find other comics and co-create a show. Pool your resources, book a space, split promo costs, and cross-promote to your respective audiences.

> **Coaching Tip:**
> **Don't do it alone**
>
> Add musicians, spoken-word artists, or even niche experts to your lineup. It makes the show more dynamic and broadens your reach.

Negotiate with Venues That Already Have an Audience

Bars, breweries, and cafés are always looking for ways to draw a crowd on slow nights.

Here's how to pitch your show:

- **Offer a low-risk proposal**—split ticket sales while they keep drink/food profits
- **Showcase your value**—explain how your show fits their vibe and brings the right crowd
- **Pitch consistency**—venues love dependable buzz. Propose a monthly or biweekly event
- **Target their slow nights**—Tuesdays or Wednesdays are perfect for a test run

Match Your Niche to the Perfect Venue

The magic happens when your comedy niche aligns with the venue and its audience. Some successful examples include:

- **Hannah Gadsby—Art Galleries**: Her art history knowledge adds depth to her comedy.
- **Doug Stanhope—House Parties:** His irreverent style shines in intimate, informal settings.
- **Kate Willett—Feminist Bookstores:** Her politically charged humor empowers audiences.
- **Gabriel Iglesias—Food Trucks:** Pairing comedy with the universal love of food trucks? Genius.

WARNING: Know your audience. Mormon family-friendly material probably doesn't belong in a tequila-fueled dive bar.

Exercise #26:
Brainstorm Venues

Take a moment to list *three unconventional venues* that would suit your brand and audience.

- Where does your target audience already spend their time?
- What kind of space fits the vibe of your show?
- Who could you collaborate with to co-host or share costs?

If you are having difficulties finding places, try using this AI prompt:

 **AI PROMPT: FIND ME A VENUE**

Paste this into ChatGPT and customize it with your info.

"I'm a comedian developing a live comedy show based on [briefly describe your niche or theme, e.g., 'nursing and hospital life' or 'dating after divorce']. I'm looking for unconventional or niche-friendly venues in [insert your city] where I could workshop a 15–60-minute show. Please suggest local venues or event spaces that align with my target audience. Prioritize venues that allow for small performances, open mics, community gatherings, or partnerships with local businesses, and have a built-in audience. Bonus if the venue already has an audience or a unique vibe that matches my show."

Example Filled-In Version:

"I'm a comedian developing a live comedy show about the chaos of middle-aged dating. I'm based in Portland, Oregon, and I'm looking for unconventional or niche-friendly venues where I could workshop a 15–60-minute comedy show. Please suggest Portland venues that attract single women over 40, such as wine bars, bookstores, yoga studios, or local wellness centers. Bonus if they host regular events or open mics."

Exercise #27:
Book a Venue!

This week, reach out to at least one potential venue. Ask for pricing or propose a partnership. Don't wait to be invited. Invite *yourself*. And don't wait until you've organized your material and feel you are "ready." Having a gig looming on your calendar is the most effective way to *stop procrastinating* and be ready.

Remember: Every gig—paid or not—is an opportunity to refine your comedy product, test a chunk, grow your audience, and build momentum.

Coaching Tip:
Your Show Is a Slow-Cooked Masterpiece

Don't expect perfection on opening night. Your show won't appear fully formed—it'll evolve from workshopping it. You'll test material at comedy clubs, ask your followers for advice, bomb in coffee shops, kill in your friend's living room, and rework it all again. Some bits will flop, others will surprise you. But piece by piece—joke by joke, story by story—your show will take shape . . . if you stay focused and don't quit.

Once you've got a good idea of your product, go to the MMBF Workbook to discover and work on the 7 P's of Promotion: Product, Place, Price, Package, Pitch, Promote, Possibility

 **Next Up:** Your POSSIBILITY

Every comedian has that moment when the pieces finally click—when your stories, your jokes, and your purpose all line up. That's when you realize your comedy was never just about laughter; it was about *becoming*.

You've shaped your product—now let's shape your perspective.

In the next chapter, we'll step into *Possibility*—the mindset that turns a career into a calling, a comic into a creator, and a dream into a reality.

ELEMENT #5: MULTIPLE REVENUE STREAMS

—— Chapter 24 ——

Becoming the Possibility of You:
The Final Mindset Shift

• • • • • • • • • • • •

*"No one is going to give you an opportunity.
You have to create it."*

—Hasan Minhaj

• • • • • • • • • • • •

Unlock the Future You've Been Pretending Isn't Possible

Step into the future self who already made it—and start living the life your comedy was meant to create.

Hey—you made it. And that's no small thing.

Some of you flew through this book, highlighter in hand, tackling every exercise like a comedy Navy SEAL. Others? You skipped a few, got stuck, lost momentum, but *still* found your way here.

However you got here—congratulations. That says a lot about you.

Because finishing a book about *making money being funny* isn't just about learning tips and tools, it's about committing to your future. It's about saying, "*I want this. I'm ready.*"

So, let's take a moment and celebrate what you've already done:

- You defined your "why" and doubled down on a niche.
- You got to know your audience and turned them into followers.
- You created your comedy product(s).
- You explored platforms, pitched yourself, and built new revenue streams.
- You took your funny seriously—and made it a business.
- And along the way, you learned a complete playbook for turning laughs into lasting income.

That's huge.

So—why aren't you rich yet?

Your Mindset Is the Gatekeeper

Here's the truth: All the strategy in the world won't help if your brain is quietly sabotaging you.

This isn't about doing more—it's about believing differently.

It's the stories you tell yourself about success.

The whispers that say, "Not you."

Time to rewrite them. Time to rewire you.

When the Tools Aren't Enough

You've hustled. You've built. You've put yourself out there.

So if you still feel stuck, you're not broken—you're just bumping up against your beliefs.

It's not because you're lazy. Or untalented. Or your dad doesn't work at Netflix.

It's because you've skipped the most important search of all: the inner one.

Your mindset quietly drives your comedy career—how high you aim, how much you charge, and whether you keep going when things get hard. You might be sitting on a gold mine of talent, but if your brain's still in struggle mode, you'll keep finding new ways to stay broke.

Let's fix that.

What You Believe Drives What You Do

Some limiting beliefs are loud and obvious:

- "I'm not good with money."
- "Nobody pays comics well."
- "It's too late for me."

But most? They're buried deep.

According to cognitive neuroscientists, only 5% of our mental activity is conscious. That means 95% of your decisions—what you charge, what you pitch, what you avoid—are being made by beliefs you might not even know you have.

Which means this: If you think you don't have limiting beliefs . . . you might just be really good at overlooking them.

You may have completed every exercise in this book. Or maybe you started strong, then fizzled out around Chapter 7 when your Inner Heckler told you your niche was "too weird" and your pitch was "cringe."

It's okay.

The fact that you're still here means you haven't given up.

And that's the thing about mindset—it's not about being perfect. It's about noticing the patterns, calling out the stories, and choosing to write a better script.

Because here's the truth:

How much money you make isn't just about talent—it's about how much you *believe* you *deserve* to make.

Every successful comic, creator, or entrepreneur I've ever met has one thing in common:

They believe they deserve to win.

Meet Your Inner Heckler

If you've ever second-guessed yourself, hesitated to post, or backed out of a bold move because you thought, "*I'm not ready*," congratulations—you've met your *Inner Heckler*.

This voice isn't new. It's just sneaky.

It shows up with perfect timing—right when you're about to do something brave.

- You submit to a comedy contest:
  IH: "You'll never win. You're not as funny as the others."
- You finally raise your prices:
  IH: "Who do you think you are? You'll lose the gig."
- You write a killer five-minute set:
  IH: "It's been done. Nobody cares."

It's exhausting. And worse, it sounds so convincing—like a parent, a teacher, or an ex who once made you feel small and called it "being realistic."

But here's the truth: That voice is not the real you.

It's not your brilliance. It's not your intuition. It's just a bad rerun.

And as a comic, you already know what to do with hecklers: *You don't let them win.*

Exercise #28: Roast Your Inner Heckler

In *The New Comedy Bible*, I teach comics how to shut down hecklers from the stage.

Now, it's time to use that skill on the heckler in your own head.

Step #1: Hear the Heckle

In Exercise #2: Create Your Comedy Career Vision, you wrote a vision of your success. Go back and read it out loud, becoming aware of that little voice that knocks you down. Write down all the reasons that voice doesn't believe in your vision, no matter how small.

Step #2: Call It Out

Say the heckles out loud:

"Oh, so you think I'm completely untalented and wasting my life?"

Step #3: Punch Back With Humor

Agree with the heckler—but blow it up with absurdity and humor.

IH: "You've gained weight."

You: "You're right. I finally cured my anorexia. Thanks for noticing—you're a real lifesaver."

Get silly. Get sharp. Get sarcastic. Make yourself laugh.
And write it down—because this is material.
Fear doesn't get the final word. You do.
In case you forgot: You're the comic. You get the last laugh.

Hack Your Brain: The Prompt That Can Rewrite Your Subconscious for Success

Let's talk about what's *really* running the show: your subconscious beliefs.

Even if you *think* you're confident, capable, and totally down to make six figures with your comedy, you might have hidden scripts quietly sabotaging your next move.

These beliefs sound like:

"Money makes people selfish."
"If I succeed, I'll lose my friends."
"If I charge more, no one will book me."
"I'm too old to start something new."

They feel like "truth," but they're just stories.

And you're a storyteller. So, let's rewrite them.

Here's the tool I personally used to change my own internal script—and it's been a total game-changer:

Exercise #29:
Reprogram Your Mind for Success

If you're ready to uncover what's *really* been holding you back, try this.

> **Open ChatGPT and enter the following prompt:**
> **Copy + Paste This Prompt:**
> *I want to identify the subconscious beliefs that are shaping my reality and stopping me from achieving my full potential. Guide me through this process with 10 deep questions, one at a time, that will help me uncover hidden fears, self-imposed limitations, and blind spots. After I answer the final question, analyze my responses as a life coach would. Tell me the recurring themes in my thinking and what's holding me back. What are the most significant mindset shifts I need to make? Then, provide me with daily affirmations and practical action steps. End with a message from my future self—the version of me who has already succeeded.*

This is your mental gym. Work out the daily affirmations and action steps. Keep the dialogue open.

Exercise #30:
Close the Loop with Your Why

Remember where you started? Back in Chapter One, you wrote down your "Why"—the reason you get up on stage, the reason you want to make money being funny, the reason laughter matters to you. Now it's time to revisit it.

Step #1: Find Your Original Why

Pull out your notes from Exercise #1: Discover Your "Why." Read it. Let yourself feel where you were back then.

Step #2: Rewrite from the Future You

Now, write a new version—but this time, from the perspective of your *future self*. The you who already made it. The headliner. The touring comic. The paid creator.

Write it as if it's already true:

"I make people laugh because…"
"My comedy matters because…"
"The world is better because I…"

Step #3: Compare the Two

Notice the shift. See how your "Why" has evolved—from a seed of hope to a full-grown vision.

Step #4: Post It Where You'll See It Daily

Put that new "Why" on your wall, your mirror, or your desktop background. Let it remind you: This isn't just a dream anymore. It's a possibility you're already manifesting.

Final Word: Step Into the Possibility of You

You've done the work. You've faced your fears. You've created something that didn't exist before—a comedy product, a brand, a vision.

But most of all, you've started becoming someone new.

Not just a comic.

Not just a creator.

But a possibility.

So what does it mean to create your future from possibility?

It means you don't need to know *how* it's all going to happen.

You don't need a perfect plan, or a spreadsheet, or a 10-step funnel.

You just need to believe in it.

Speak it.

Take one small step toward it.

And then another.

Martin Luther King Jr. didn't say, "*I have a plan.*"

He said, "*I have a dream.*"

He painted a picture of a world that didn't exist yet—and it still moves people to action decades later. That's the power of possibility.

You began this book with your "*why.*"

The reason you get on stage. The reason you believe laughter can heal.

For me? It's my sister.

Every time I step on a stage, I picture her in the back row in her wheelchair—smiling, uplifted, seen. She reminds me that this work matters. That humor isn't just entertainment—it's medicine.

That's the purpose I carry with me.

And it's the purpose I now pass on to you.

You are a gift to this world.

You have the power to turn your own struggles into laughter—and in doing so, remind others that *they* are powerful too, no matter what they've been through.

This journey isn't easy. I still backslide.

Just last month, I was offered a gig for more money than I've ever made—and I was flooded with imposter syndrome. Couldn't sleep. Couldn't focus. My inner heckler was screaming.

But I kept going.

Because the work is hard—but it's possible.

And now, you've done the most challenging part:

You've imagined the version of you who already made it.

You've let AI describe the life you want.

Now it's time to step into that life.

That version of you isn't just a fantasy.

That's *you*—without fear.

That's *you*—fully expressed.

That's *you*—as a powerful force for joy, connection, and prosperity.

So, carry that version with you.

Let that vision speak when you're scared.

Let it pitch when you want to shrink.

Let it walk into every room like you belong—because you do.

That vision is the possibility of you.

Now go live it.

And . . . the next time your Inner Heckler says, "Who do you think you are?"—just smile, grab the mic, and say, "The headliner, bitch."

The Comedian's Hub

• • • • • • • • • • • •

"Now that you've told your Inner Heckler to sit down and shut up ... let's keep the party going."

• • • • • • • • • • • •

Where Funny Becomes Profitable

Whether you're just starting out or ready to turn your comedy into cash flow, **The Comedian's Hub at JudyCarter.com** is your one-stop shop for tools, inspiration, and next steps.

You'll find everything I've created to help you *make money being funny*—from books and workbooks to workshops, coaching, and digital resources. What's new changes, but the goal stays the same: **to help you build a creative life that pays.**

Inside The Hub, you might discover:

- Interactive workbooks and guided exercises
- Mindset tools for overcoming fear and self-doubt
- Global Online and live workshops
- Audio series and on-demand classes
- Resources to grow your comedy brand and audience

If you're ready to stop waiting for permission and start profiting from your talent, head to JudyCarter.com

https://www.judycarter.com/resources-gallore

Because the tools might change—but the mission never will...
Helping you turn your funny into freedom.

Other Books by Judy Carter

Standup Comedy: The Book
(Dell Publishing)

The Homo Handbook
(Simon & Schuster)

The Comedy Bible
(Simon & Schuster)

*The Message of You:
Turn Your Life Story into a Money-Making Speaking Career*
(St. Martin's Press)

*The Message of You Journal:
Finding Extraordinary Stories in an Ordinary Day*
(Comedy Workshops Publishing)

The Comedy Bible Workbook
(Simon & Schuster)

The New Comedy Bible
(Comedy Workshops Publishing)

The Making Money Being Funny Workbook
(Comedy Workshops Publishing)

Acknowledgments

Writing a book takes a village—preferably one that knows how to laugh. I began this journey over three years ago, meeting regularly with the talented comic Diana Hong, whom I first encountered at an L.A. open mic where the audience was the comics. I spent far more than forty days and forty nights wandering through ideas until, with the help of my BFF, the insightful Laura Pelegrin—whose Ph.D. in psychology helped me crack the "Formula"—I finally found the path forward.

My first editor, Henry DeVries of Indie Books International, who also published *The New Comedy Bible*, kept me on schedule and on track.

And then SJ Hodges—who worked her magic on my book *The Message of You*—came aboard and shaped this manuscript into the book you're holding. I absolutely could not have reached this finish line without her.

Special thanks to Sybil Sage, Dean Lewis, Dawn Xanklin, Jackie Joy, and Jeffrey Jay for their sharp comedic contributions, and to Danielle Thorpe for finding me designers to bring the cover to life. Special thanks to Nicole Blaine at the Crow for creating a supportive club for welcoming all comedians of diversity and giving me a stage to take chances.

Thanks to everyone who joined the Zoom readings and punched things up, including Andrea Caspari, Bernice Ye, Terill Jackson, Helaine Witt, and Darryn "Dutch" Martin.

And deep gratitude to the many generous people who read chapters out loud to me and offered suggestions, including Asta D'Errico, Alana Johnson, Alexa Speaks, Alexa Viruet, Alice Niu, Bernice Ye, Bonita Joy Yoder, Carla Ulbrich, Ceci Walken, Conni Eckstein, Cory Clark, David Uribe, Dominic Scimeca, Elizabeth Randall, Elizabeth Swaney, Felicia Hollins, Frank King, Ginger Claremohr, Glenn Garry, Greg Owens, Kartikey Shivkant Mishra, Jade Wong, Janesh Rahlan, Jeff Jackson, Jeff Kothe, Jennifer Johnson, Joel Marshall, John Alexander Ball, Kathy Guest, Kim Wadsworth, Laurie Ayer, Lisa Jones, Marrielle Monte, Mike J. Toy, Molly Hamilton, Paula Harrington-Hill, Qihan (Molly) Chen, Susan Quintanar, Susanna Allen, Terill Jackson, Tosin Arowojolu, Tracey B. Simon and Wilbur Bowen.

Thanks to PR guru Margot Black for your expert support.

To all of you—thank you for lending your voices, your humor, and your brain cells. You turned what could have been a lonely writer's slog into a community project filled with laughter, heart, and the occasional "Are you sure you want to keep that joke?" I'm forever grateful . . . and if this book becomes a bestseller, I promise to remember all of you in my acceptance speech—right after Oprah.

Finally, my unending gratitude to my first editor, Chuck Adams, who took a chance on a young writer and launched my career as an author. You are always with me every time I write—like a literary guardian angel, only with stronger opinions and better grammar.

Made in the USA
Coppell, TX
25 February 2026

72306464R00122